The Forgotten Luther II

The Forgotten Luther II

Reclaiming the Church's Public Witness

RYAN P. CUMMING, EDITOR

FORTRESS PRESS
MINNEAPOLIS

THE FORGOTTEN LUTHER II

Reclaiming the Church's Public Witness

Scripture quotations are from the New Revised Standard Version Bible © 1989 Division of Christian Education of the National Council of the Churches of Christ in the United States of America. Used by permission.

Verses from "The Canticle of the Turning" (*Evangelical Lutheran Worship* 723) by Rory Cooney © 1990, GIA Publications, Inc. All rights reserved. Used by permission.

Cover image: Background texture: Miodrag Kitanović; City vector: mspoint
Cover design: Joe Reinke

Print ISBN: 978-1-5064-4708-7
eBook ISBN: 978-1-5064-4709-4

The paper used in this publication meets the minimum requirements of American National Standard for Information Sciences — Permanence of Paper for Printed Library Materials, ANSI Z329.48-1984.

Manufactured in the U.S.A.

Contents

Abbreviations

BC   *The Book of Concord*. Edited by Robert Kolb and Timothy J. Wengert. Minneapolis: Fortress Press, 2000

LW   *Luther's Works* [American edition]. Edited by Helmut Lehmann and Jaroslav Pelikan. 55 vols. Philadelphia: Fortress Press; St. Louis: Concordia, 1955–1986

TAL   *The Annotated Luther*. Edited by Hans J. Hillerbrand, Kirsi I. Stjerna, and Timothy J. Wengert. 6 vols. Minneapolis: Fortress Press, 2015–2017

WA   *Luthers Werke: Kritische Gesamtausgabe* [Schriften]. 73 vols. Weimar: H. Böhlau, 1883–2009

Introduction

CONRAD BRAATEN AND PAUL WEE

He has shown strength with his arm;
    he has scattered the proud in the thoughts of their hearts.
He has brought down the powerful from their thrones
    and lifted up the lowly;
he has filled the hungry with good things
    and sent the rich away empty.

—Luke 1:51–53

From the halls of power to the fortress tower,
not a stone will be left on stone.
Let the king beware for your justice tears
every tyrant from his throne.
The hungry poor shall weep no more,
for the food they can never earn;
These are tables spread, ev'ry mouth be fed,
for the world is about to turn.

—From "Canticle of the Turning"
(Evangelical Lutheran Worship 723, stanza 3)

ORIGINS OF THIS STUDY: CONGREGATIONS IN MISSION

When the Forgotten Luther project began in 2015, we were caught off guard by the enthusiastic response as readers encountered a Luther they never knew. Discovering Luther's initiative to share wealth and provide medical care through the common chest, for example, surprised many readers. Did Martin Luther actually do that? The feedback from many congregations that participated in study programs based on *The Forgotten Luther: Reclaiming the Social-Economic Dimension of the Reformation* (Lutheran University Press, 2016) encouraged us to hold another symposium and produce this second volume. We do so with gratitude to many congregations and to ELCA World Hunger, a ministry of the Evangelical Lutheran Church in America.

What caught the attention of congregations? Quite simply it was the realization that Martin Luther, in collaboration with the civil authorities in Wittenberg and Saxony, initiated far-reaching, government-supported economic reforms that promoted access to food, medical care, education, and sufficient resources for all people to survive with dignity in old age. The legacy of this collaboration finds one expression in the economic and social policies of several European and Nordic countries today. Equally surprising to many lay leaders and pastors was the realization that Luther's actions on behalf of the poor were directly linked to the egalitarianism implied in the central teaching of the church, justification by grace through faith.

The implications of congregations' rediscovery of the Reformation's socioeconomic dimension are immense. They support a faith-based commitment to the common good, something that has been largely obscured in the church's concern—justifiable but at times one-sided—to proclaim the central teaching of justification for the individual. The affirmation of the Reformation's socioeconomic dimension is especially significant in our own day, as we witness an increasing unevenness in the distribution of the wealth of the earth.

THE PRESENT REALITY: THE WORLD IS ABOUT TO TURN

The fact that we are living at a time of convulsive and unprecedented change is reflected in a favorite hymn of many Christian communities, "Canticle of the Turning." Though people in every historical era witness change, the speed and extent of the present transformation sets our period apart. Welcome advances in medical research and technology are countered by immense threats to the integrity of human community and to the creation itself. The intensified political posturing between nuclear powers has created a climate of considerable apprehension. People in the United States express a growing unhappiness with the polarization within the country and its governing bodies.

In the midst of tumultuous change and the anxiety that accompanies it, congregations continue to proclaim steadfast faith in the hopeful transformation God is creating in our midst. They are asking the not-so-innocent question Confessing Church theologian Dietrich Bonhoeffer raised amid the earth-shaking changes taking place with the rise of the Third Reich: "Who is Jesus Christ for us today?" They are also proclaiming—in a new idiom—an age-old message of hope in a God who, in the words of Rory Cooney, is turning the world around.

Though the nations rage from age to age,
we remember who holds us fast:
God's mercy must deliver us
from the conqueror's crushing grasp.
This saving word that our forebears heard
is the promise which holds us bound,
till the spear and rod can be crushed by God,
who is turning the world around.
("Canticle of the Turning," *Evangelical Lutheran Worship* 723, stanza 4)

THE PURPOSE OF THIS STUDY: EMPOWERING THE CHURCH TO SPEAK

At this critical time in history, the Forgotten Luther project seeks to provide lay and rostered leaders with resources for shaping a viable response to some formidable challenges.

- How are we to preach the gospel faithfully in a way that speaks realistically to our situation?

- What is the shape of mission today?

- How is the church to respond when policies or actions of the government appear to be at odds with its message?

The study's point of departure is the theological heritage of Martin Luther and his conviction that government is responsible to God for maintaining peace and good order and for ensuring that no person is hungry or in want. These essays seek to make clear how Luther gave expression to his convictions in his historical context, and how they might serve as a resource in ours. They show, as Mary Jane Haemig documents, how the lives of the common people of Luther's day—girls as well as boys, women as well as men—were dramatically changed not only through access to the vernacular Scripture and the catechism, and through participation in worship, but also through publicly financed education.

In his essay on racism in culture and the church, Anthony Bateza interrogates the legacy of Lutheran responses to racism. After defining both individual racism and structural racism, Bateza draws insights from Luther's theology of baptism and confession that lead faith communities to respond effectively to the many forms of this sin. To make his case, he creatively puts Luther in conversation with twentieth-century writer James Baldwin.

Far from idealizing Luther, however, the authors of these essays make clear the ways in which the Reformation heritage—indeed, Luther himself—at times contradicted the very principles on which the reform movement was built. Kirsi Stjerna's essay, for example, confronts Luther's vitriolic attack against the Jews, as well as the way his writings were used to support the racist policies of the Third Reich. In the church of Luther today, she maintains, there can be "no tolerance for anti-Semitism."

Historically, there have been times when many in the church supported the absolutist claims of the state, such as National Socialism in Germany in the 1930s. At other times, people following some forms of pietism have encouraged the church's withdrawal from engagement in political life altogether. In her essay, Wanda Deifelt traces the roots of such noninvolvement to the unbiblical dualisms that have drawn a sharp line between the soul and the body, the spiritual and the material.

In the face of both extremes, Carter Lindberg affirms Luther's call for a critical, public witness by the church. This witness means, on the one hand, rejecting all attempts to equate the kingdom of God with a political program or institution and, on the other, affirming the church's responsible participation in political life. It is within the context of the congregation that questions must continually be raised: When should the church support the state's agenda? When resist? When engage in critical but constructive cooperation? How can the gospel of Jesus Christ shape our response today?

WRESTLING WITH THE HERITAGE: THE UNIQUE ROLE OF THE CONGREGATION

With many of our colleagues in parish ministry, we are invigorated by the challenge to speak the Word faithfully in our cultural and political contexts. This witness always entails risk. When we have learned that people thought our words were too "political" or partisan, transgressing the "separation of church and state" or confusing "gospel with law," we have sought to listen. At the end of the day, we have gone back to Holy Scripture and to the theology of the church that has been informed by Luther's teachings. We continue to welcome honest debate rooted in theological reflection and ethical deliberation.

With disastrous consequences, history has shown that when dialogue, deliberation, and debate are stifled for the sake of an artificial "harmony," the church faces a lose-lose situation. Spiritual growth and learning cease, and the congregation becomes a mirror of society. This is one of the lessons to be drawn from the essays in this book. The church's public witness is central to the church's identity, the formation of its members, and its relationship to both the world and to God.

For his part, Luther, who affirmed the role of reason in efforts to work toward the common good, gives us plenty to think about and discuss concerning the church's public witness in our world today. Lutheran theologians participating in the 2015 symposium, "The Forgotten Luther: Reclaiming the Social-Economic Dimension of the Reformation," as well as those who contribute to this volume, show us a Luther who, in the name of Christian freedom and God's grace, pulls us out of the pew and into the forum of public discourse. The Christian gospel does have a public witness. What better place to give shape to that witness than in the congregation!

As you begin this study on the church's public witness, remember a few things. First, if our Christian faith does not inform our being in the world (our vote, our works of love, our advocacy, and our public witness), our being in the world (opinions, fads, and worldviews) will shape our faith. When that happens, congregations become simple reflections of the prevailing culture.

Second, in this congregational work, we are not alone. We do not need to reinvent the wheel. The ELCA as a whole has a long history of enabling people of diverse opinions, perspectives, and expertise to contribute in the development of endorsed statements of social advocacy. These statements, as you will learn from the chapter contributed by Amy Reumann, are thoughtfully developed, not as a "law" but as a guide to advocacy and a foundation for study and deliberation in the congregations of our church.

What might happen if our congregations became settings where people together wrestle with Scripture, our theological heritage, and Christian ethics to shape our witness in the world? We hope you enjoy this study. Let it be a journey of "faith, active in love."

1.

Reclaiming Luther's Public Witness on Church, State, and War

CARTER LINDBERG

Martin Luther's writings that speak truth to power have not been a significant part of recent commemorations of the Reformation. Luther's contribution to the church's public witness remains largely forgotten except for the traditional image of a lone hero defying emperor and pope at the Diet of Worms. I am reminded of a comment I heard in graduate school from Sidney Mead. Well known for his studies of religion in America, Mead, a Unitarian, remarked that Lutherans in America reminded him of a football team in a huddle. They might be discussing something important, but all we see are their backsides.

About the same time I heard Mead, I was reading studies by the Methodist Luther scholar Gordon Rupp. Rupp cheered me up a bit by noting that there is nothing quite so wrong with Lutherans that a good dose of Luther might not help.[1] More recently Mark Noll, a leading evangelical historical theologian, has called for the public witness of Lutherans as a corrective to American Christendom: "American Evangelicals need the Lutherans, and we need them now."[2] If a Unitarian, a Methodist, and an evangelical think Luther might have something to offer, perhaps we should pay attention.

1. Mead's works include Sidney Mead, *The Lively Experiment: The Shaping of Christianity in America* (New York: Harper & Row, 1963); and Mead, *The Nation with the Soul of a Church* (New York: Harper & Row, 1975). Among Rupp's many studies is Gordon Rupp, *The Righteousness of God: Luther Studies* (London: Hodder & Stoughton, 1953).

2. Mark Noll, "An Evangelical Protestant Perspective," *Word & World* 11, no. 3 (1991): 312–15, 312; Noll, "The Lutheran Difference," *First Things*, February 1992, 31–40; Noll, "Ethnic, American, or Lutheran? Dilemmas for a Historic Confession in the New World," *Lutheran Theological Seminary Bulletin* 71, no. 1 (1991): 17–43.

Noll sees Luther's theology as an antidote to the pervasive American piety of achievement with its moralistic sanctification of America's nationalist ideology, and to the evangelical "predilection for confusing the history of the United States with the history of salvation."[3] Knowingly or not, Noll echoes Dietrich Bonhoeffer's assessment of Christianity in America as "Protestantism without Reformation."[4] Bonhoeffer, profoundly influenced by Luther's theology, asserted that the church in America, as is evident in so many sermons, reduces the gospel to a moralization that confuses private and public morality.[5] Douglas John Hall likewise comments: "There is no better illustration of the triviality of private morality with which the churches of this continent have occupied themselves than that it had so little influence on the *public* morality that has shaped our peoples' attitudes toward nature, other races, the poor, economic policies, and women."[6] To paraphrase Jesus, we have become adept at straining out gnats and swallowing camels, while neglecting "the weightier matters of the law: justice and mercy and faith" (Matt 23:23). We need only glance at the United States' health, social security, taxation, and Pentagon policies to see our corporate "greed and self-indulgence" (v. 26). The slogan "America first" is but a more recent expression of American exceptionalism, the triumphalism that God is on our side.

All of which brings us to an insightful essay by Conrad Braaten titled "The Elephant in the Sanctuary."[7] The "elephant" is civil religion, the identification of religious belief with the prevailing national ideology.[8] Writing in the wake of the Persian Gulf Wars, Braaten notes the congregational turmoil reaching back to the Vietnam War as pastors and

3. Mark Noll, "What Lutherans Have to Offer Public Theology," *Lutheran Quarterly* 22, no. 2 (2008): 125–36, 126.

4. *Dietrich Bonhoeffer Works*, vol. 15, *Theological Education Underground: 1937–1940*, ed. Victoria J. Barnett, trans. Claudia D. Bergmann, Scott A. Moore, and Peter Frick (Minneapolis: Fortress Press, 2011), 438–62.

5. Michael P. DeJonge, *Bonhoeffer's Reception of Luther* (Oxford: Oxford University Press, 2017), 122–23, cf. 261: "Bonhoeffer was a creative, dynamic participant in the Lutheran theological tradition"; and 219: "Bonhoeffer's early resistance writings are steeped in Lutheran resistance resources." See also Michael P. DeJonge, "Martin Luther, Dietrich Bonhoeffer, and Political Theologies," *Oxford Research Encyclopedias*, 2016, https://tinyurl.com/y7eruaw3.

6. Douglas John Hall, *Lighten Our Darkness: Toward an Indigenous Theology of the Cross* (Philadelphia: Westminster, 1976), 216.

7. Conrad Braaten, "The Elephant in the Sanctuary," *Congregations*, Fall 2003, https://tinyurl.com/ya2pt6tm.

8. American civil religion blossomed in the 1950s, conflating evangelicalism and capitalism with the motto "in God we trust" on money and postage. See Kevin M. Kruse, *One Nation under God: How Corporate America Invented Christian America* (New York: Basic Books, 2015); Frances Fitzgerald, *The Evangelicals: The Struggle to Shape America* (New York: Simon & Schuster, 2017); and Chris Hedges, *American Fascists: The Christian Right and the War on America* (New York: Free Press, 2006).

parishioners wrestled with issues of justice and peace. The endowment of ethnic and national aspirations with the ultimate blessing of God is, of course, not uniquely American.[9] Even a cursory reading of the Bible reveals the prevalence of "court prophets" who sanctify national goals. Hence the biblical refrain to beware of false prophets who always claim that God is on our side. True prophets, as we all know, are not well received. When folks like Amos inform us that "the day of the Lord" will not be our triumph but our destruction (see Amos 5), the usual response is to shoot the messenger. Most pastors soon learn that prophetic sermons are a key to early retirement. Luther knew this as well. By the Diet of Worms, he assumed early retirement would be permanent retirement!

Before launching into Luther as a resource for public witness, it is important to remember that Luther understood himself to be primarily a pastor and theologian. His theology was revolutionary but not a theology of revolution. His pastoral-theological breakthrough that the righteousness of God is "pure gift without reciprocation" has been described as "a paradigm shift *par excellence*," "a fundamental 'system-crashing' departure from medieval religiosity."[10] Luther clearly identified the radical nature of God's gift in his discussion of Hebrews 9:17: God names us in his last will and testament, and dies to make it effective.

> You would have to spend a long time polishing your shoes, preening and primping to attain an inheritance, if you had no letter and seal with which to prove your right to it. But if you [are named in the will], it must be given to you, even though you were scaly, scabby, stinking, and most filthy.[11]

Thus Luther asserts that because we are named in God's last will and testament, we may be certain of God's promise of salvation.

> This is why our theology is certain: it snatches us away from ourselves and places us outside ourselves, so that we do not depend on our own strength, conscience, experience, person, or works but depend on that which is outside ourselves, that is, on the promise and truth of God which cannot deceive.[12]

This theology initiated and advanced his political-social ethics.

9. A century and a half ago, Søren Kierkegaard penned one of the most scathing critiques of civil religion in his attack on Danish Lutheranism, *Attack upon "Christendom"* (Boston: Beacon, 1956).

10. Hans Küng, *Great Christian Thinkers* (New York: Continuum, 1995), 142 (emphasis original). Berndt Hamm, *The Early Luther: Stages in a Reformation Reorientation* (Grand Rapids: Eerdmans, 2014), 31, see also 237, 255; Hamm, "Martin Luther's Revolutionary Theology of Pure Gift without Reciprocation," *Lutheran Quarterly* 29, no. 2 (2015): 125–61.

11. LW 35:88; cf. LW 36:38.

12. LW 26:387.

There is no theological teaching of Luther that is politically innocent. His theology and politics must be distinguished but never separated. Luther himself is thus the first and best witness that the so-called "Two-Kingdoms-Doctrine" does not lead to political abstinence but exactly the opposite: the world as a whole with its problems and decisions is now discovered as the subject of Christian responsibility.[13]

So, Luther concluded his famous 1520 tract *The Freedom of a Christian*: "[A] Christian lives not in himself, but in Christ and in his neighbor. Otherwise he is not a Christian. He lives in Christ through faith, in his neighbor through love."[14] Luther's

> politics is genuinely theological, in that it is a politics lived out of faith in the God who alone judges and justifies, thus placing necessary restrictions on the tendency of politics to absorb all of human life, as would be the case in the thinking of [those] . . . who seek in place of a full-blooded Christianity a civil religion.[15]

How then did Luther reclaim the church's public witness? What clues does he offer us? In brief, Luther's "paradigm shift" smashed the civil religion of his day, the medieval *corpus Christianum*, through appeal to the biblical witness and to reason. In *The Forgotten Luther: Reclaiming the Social-Economic Dimension of the Reformation*, we explored how Luther did this in relation to the political economy. Here I will sketch how Luther publicly addressed governing officials and then summarize his reflections on war as a kind of case study.

ADDRESSING RULERS

One of the ways Luther addressed governing authorities is known as a *Fürstenspiegel* (mirror for princes). This is an ancient literary genre that critiques royal power by raising a mirror to its excesses and advises the ruler on appropriate governance. An early biblical example is 1 Samuel 8:11–18, a dreadful divine warning of what life will be like if Israel chooses to have a king.[16] Luther's writings are filled with biblical counsel

13. Günter Brakelmann, *Martin Luther—Beiträge zu seinen Verständnis* (Kamen: Spenner, 2012), 154.

14. LW 31:371.

15. Michael Laffin, *The Promise of Martin Luther's Political Theology: Freeing Luther from the Modern Political Narrative* (London: Bloomsbury T&T Clark, 2016), 3–4, summarizes the "modern political narrative" of Luther as "apolitical and essentially quietistic at best or antipolitical and authoritarian at worst."

16. Jonathan Kaplan, "1 Samuel 8:11–18 as a 'Mirror for Princes,'" *Journal of Biblical Literature* 131, no. 4 (2012), 625–42.

for rulers. An early example is *To the Christian Nobility of the German Nation Concerning the Improvement of the Christian Estate* (1520).[17] Well aware that he will be thought presumptuous for venturing to call out social and economic injustice, Luther assumes the well-worn guise of court jester to bell the cat and speak truth to power.

> More than once a fool has spoken wisely, and wise men have often been errant fools. . . . Moreover, since I am not only a fool, but also a sworn doctor of Holy Scripture, I am glad for the opportunity to fulfill my doctor's oath, even in the guise of a fool.[18]

A more direct treatise followed in 1523: *Temporal Authority: To What Extent It Should Be Obeyed*.[19] Based on sermons before princes, this tract captures Luther's rejection of medieval "civil religion."

> God has ordained two governments: the spiritual, by which the Holy Spirit produces Christians and righteous people under Christ, and the temporal, which restrains the wicked so that—no thanks to them—they are obliged to keep still and to maintain outward peace.[20]

> [Since] Christians are few and far between . . . it is out of the question that there should be a common Christian government . . . over a single country or any considerable body of people, for the wicked always outnumber the good.[21]

Luther addresses this issue further in other writings.

> Christians are not needed for secular authority. It is not necessary for the emperor to be a saint. It is not necessary for him to be a Christian to rule. It is sufficient for the emperor to possess reason.[22]

> God has placed human civil life under the dominion of natural reason which has enough ability to rule physical things. Reason and experience together teach . . . how to do everything else that belongs to sustaining life here on

---

17. Although the title in LW 44 uses "Reform," the German term is "Improvement" (*Besserung*); cf. Martin Luther, *Studienausgabe*, ed. Hans-Ulrich Delius, 6 vols (Berlin: Verlagsanstalt, 1979–1999), 2:89–95.

18. LW 44:123–24. On Luther as "court jester," see Eric W. Gritsch, *The Wit of Martin Luther* (Minneapolis: Fortress Press, 2006).

19. LW 45:75–129. Cf. the German edition with introduction and notes in StA 3:27–71; Albrecht Beutel, "Biblischer Text und theologische Theoriebildung in Luthers Schrift 'Von weltlicher Oberkeit, wie weit man ihr Gehorsam schuldig sei' (1523)," in *Reflektierte Religion: Beiträge zur Geschichte des Protestantismus* (Tübingen: Mohr Siebeck, 2007), 21–46; Brakelmann, *Martin Luther*, 44–69.

20. LW 45:91; cf. LW 13:193–95.

21. LW 45:91.

22. WA 27:418,2–4.

earth. These powers have been graciously bestowed by God upon human reason, and we need not look to Scripture for advice in such temporal matters. God has seen to it that even the heathen is blessed with the gift of reason to help him live his daily life.[23]

Reason and experience are instrumental to promoting the common good and thus provide perspective on the law. So Luther argued, for example, against mandatory sentencing. It is better to punish too little than too much, "for it is always better to let a scoundrel live than to put a godly man to death. The world has plenty of scoundrels . . . but godly men are scarce."[24] Luther's point could be extrapolated to current issues such as immigration and the "Dreamers." "God made the secular government subordinate and subject to reason, because it is to have no jurisdiction over the welfare of souls or things of eternal value but only over physical and temporal goods."[25] William Lazareth emphasizes this point:

> Rather than attempt any naïve and fruitless "Christianization" of the fallen social structures in the community, Christ's followers should dedicate their consecrated brains to learn even from conscientious pagans how best to live their daily lives so as to achieve the most equitable society possible under human reason, law, and order.[26]

Luther's 1521 *Commentary on the Magnificat* was addressed to John Frederick (1503–1554), the nephew of Elector Frederick the Wise.[27] At first glance, the Magnificat would seem to be a good and safe text to use when advising a prince. Medieval theology had long praised Mary for her humility. According to the prevailing medieval interpretation, she was chosen to be the mother of God and elevated to become Queen of Heaven because of her virtue. Luther, however, realized that Mary's "lowliness" is not the virtue of humility but actual poverty.[28] Luther

---

23. WA 16:353,27–33.

24. LW 45:104–5; cf. 118–29.

25. Martin Luther, *Commentary on Psalm 101* (1535), LW 13:143–224. This *Fürstenspiegel* was addressed to Prince John Frederick, to whom Luther had also dedicated his *Commentary on the Magnificat* (1521). Cf. Michael Basse, "Ideale Herrschaft und politische Realität. Luthers Auslegung des 101. Psalms im Kontext von Spätmittelalter und Reformation," *Zeitschrift für Kirchengeschichte* 114 (2003): 45–71.

26. William Lazareth, *Christians in Society: Luther, the Bible, and Social Ethics* (Minneapolis: Fortress Press, 2001), 170. See also Carter Lindberg, "'Christianization' and Luther on the Early Profit Economy," in *The Reformation as Christianization: Essays on Scott Hendrix's Christianization Thesis*, ed. Anna Marie Johnson and John A. Maxfield (Tübingen: Mohr Siebeck, 2012), 49–78.

27. LW 21:295–358.

28. LW 21:312–17. The exegetical foundation for Luther's rejection of the monastic piety of humility was provided by Erasmus's 1519 *Annotationes* to his edition of the Greek New Testament, *Novum Instrumentum*. The Greek text does not speak of the virtue of humility but of

rejects the spiritualization of poverty and addresses poverty as a socioeconomic condition to be remedied.[29] Luther gets the radical message of the Bible: the last shall be first, and the first shall be last. The gospel turns the world upside down! In the terms used by liberation theologians, God's choice of Mary expresses God's preferential option for the poor.[30] Rulers are to be warned that "power, riches, and honor . . . form so strong an incentive to presumption and smugness" that the ruler "forgets God and does not care about his subjects," and "becomes a beast, does whatever he pleases, and is a ruler in name, but a monster in deed." Rulers need to be ever mindful that "God is the kind of Lord who does nothing but exalt those of low degree and put down the mighty from their thrones, in short, break what is whole and make whole what is broken."[31] Beyond providing biblically based advice to rulers, Luther was not at all hesitant to speak truth to power, often in quite sharp terms.

LUTHER ON WAR

Military conflict raged as much in Luther's day as in ours, when "the military-industrial complex" (per President Eisenhower) rules the world.[32] War remains one of the great "rackets" by which vast wealth is created "at the expense of the very many."[33] Just as German industrialists

a literally poor social condition. See Christof Burger, *Tradition und Neubeginn: Martin Luther in seinen frühen Jahren* (Tübingen: Mohr Siebeck, 2014), 134–36; Heiko A. Oberman, *The Harvest of Medieval Theology: Gabriel Biel and Late Medieval Nominalism* (Cambridge, MA: Harvard University Press, 1963), 301–2, 306, 320–22.

29. See Paul Wee and Carter Lindberg, eds., *The Forgotten Luther: Reclaiming the Social-Economic Dimension of the Reformation* (Minneapolis: Lutheran University Press, 2016).

30. Bonhoeffer, influenced by Luther, makes the same point of viewing history "from below, from the perspective of the outcast, the suspects, the maltreated, the powerless, the oppressed, the reviled—in short, from the perspective of those who suffer." *Dietrich Bonhoeffer Works*, vol. 8, *Letters and Papers from Prison*, ed. John W. de Gruchy, trans. Reinhard Krauss, Nancy Lukens, Lisa E. Dahill, and Isabel Best (Minneapolis: Fortress Press, 2010), 52, cited by Jenny Anne Wright, "Living with a Conscience?," in *A Spoke in the Wheel: The Political in the Theology of Dietrich Bonhoeffer*, ed. Kirsten Busch Nielsen, Rolf Karolus Wüstenberg, and Jens Zimmermann (Gütersloh: Gütersloher Verlagshaus, 2014), 247–56, 253. See Walter Altmann, *Luther and Liberation: A Latin American Perspective* (Minneapolis: Fortress Press, 1992).

31. LW 21:298–99. The commentary was reprinted eight times in the next five years along with two printings of a Latin translation (LW 21:XIX). See Christoph Burger, "Luther als geistlicher Ratgeber Johann Friedrichs von Sachsen im Widmungsbrief seiner Auslegung des 'Magnifikat' (1520/21)," in *Orientierung für das Leben: Kirchliche Bildung und Politik in Spätmittelalter, Reformation und Neuzeit*, ed. Patrik Mähling (Berlin: LIT, 2010), 81–92.

32. Dwight D. Eisenhower's "Farewell Address to the Nation" (January 17, 1961) warned against the influence of the military-industrial complex wielding undue economic and political power. See Wikipedia, "Eisenhower's Farewell Address," last modified August 26, 2018, https://tinyurl.com/ztbwm47.

33. Brigadier General Smedley Butler, *War Is a Racket* (1935; repr., Los Angeles: Feral House, 2003).

welcomed Hitler's arms economy, so our country promotes arms sales throughout the world. War is the alchemy of turning blood into gold.[34]

Whenever the topic of Luther and war arises, the cliché that Luther was a toady of the princes is soon to follow. The "received wisdom" is that Luther's writings on submitting to authorities (who are put in place by God) set in motion a German-specific pathology of obedience that inevitably led to Christian passivity before National Socialism. Such nonsense has had an incredibly long shelf life, stretching from the shrill rhetoric of Luther's contemporary Thomas Müntzer's charge that Luther was a tool of the princes through Ernst Troeltsch's argument that Luther split public and personal morality, thus disposing Lutheranism to political absolutism. Within academia Troeltsch's position was perpetuated by Reinhold Niebuhr. In popular culture these charges are present in William Shirer's nearly omnipresent book *The Rise and Fall of the Third Reich*.[35]

The caricature of Luther as the poster child for quietism at best and Fascism at worst has been debunked by Peter Blickle, in *Obedient Germans? A Rebuttal*; Uwe Siemon-Netto, in *The Fabricated Luther: The Rise and Fall of the Shirer Myth*; David Whitford, in *Tyranny and Resistance: The Magdeburg Confession and the Lutheran Tradition*; Hans-Ulrich Wehler, in "The Goldhagen Controversy: Agonizing Problems, Scholarly Failure and the Political Dimension"; and most recently the 2017 study by Michael DeJonge, *Bonhoeffer's Reception of Luther*.[36] Blickle "challenges directly one of the most cherished of modern dogmas about the political behavior of the Germans: that they are peculiarly susceptible, because of their historical experience, to passivity toward authoritarian regimes." Blickle states, "No one ever gave the communal principle a more apt theological foundation than did Luther."[37] But

---

34. Dieter Beese et al., eds., *Günter Brakelmann: Ein Theologe in Konflikten seiner Zeit. Biografische Interviews* (Berlin: LIT, 2006), 159. Aaron Mehta, "US Clears Record Total for Arms Sales in FY17," *Defense News*, September 13, 2017, https://tinyurl.com/y7vcqadc (75.9 billion); "U.S. arms sales jump 25 percent in FY 2017," *Reuters*, November 29, 2017, https://tinyurl.com /yarqw3st.

35. William Shirer, *The Rise and Fall of the Third Reich* (New York: Simon & Schuster, 1960). See Uwe Siemon-Netto, *The Fabricated Luther: The Rise and Fall of the Shirer Myth* (St. Louis: Concordia, 1995).

36. Peter Blickle, *Obedient Germans? A Rebuttal: A New View of German History* (Charlottesville: University Press of Virginia, 1997), Siemon-Netto, *Fabricated Luther*; David Whitford, *Tyranny and Resistance: The Magdeburg Confession and the Lutheran Tradition* (St. Louis: Concordia, 2001); Hans-Ulrich Wehler, "The Goldhagen Controversy: Agonizing Problems, Scholarly Failure and the Political Dimension," *German History* 15, no. 1 (1997): 80–91; see 88: "Goldhagen's scholarship is actually an unashamed reversion to the state of play in 1950 (when the prevailing slogan was 'From Luther to Hitler')."

37. Blickle, *Obedient Germans*, xiii, 88.

already some sixty years before Blickle's argument, Peter Drucker had exposed Nazism and Fascism as totalitarian temptations rooted in the modern economic world, not the German character.[38] Siemon-Netto effectively interprets Luther's theology of the two realms as a bulwark against the utopian and dystopian efforts of modern regimes to promote their political visions no matter the cost in lives and treasure. Whitford provides a historical-theological analysis of Luther's writings and their influence on the seminal expression of theologically grounded resistance to authority—the 1550 Magdeburg Confession. This confession by the Lutherans of Magdeburg, taken up by their followers who struggled to defend the freedom of the church against early imperial absolutism, influenced subsequent theological-political resistance movements.[39]

Without solid theological foundation and direction, the church will tend to take on the mores of the civil religion of its context; without a confession of faith, the church will have little to say in a time of crisis. The Nazis knew this better than many Christians then and now. When Hitler and his National Socialist Party seized power, they asserted support for "positive Christianity," that is, churches that serve the state. Few seemed to realize the Nazi intention to co-opt the churches with a national ideology. Many in the churches were seduced by Hitler's propaganda of family values, national identity, and the promise to make Germany great again. When the church forgets its confessions, it runs the danger of no longer knowing what it believes. What the church believes, teaches, and confesses is the community's affirmation that "not anything goes." It was, therefore, no accident that, when faced by National Socialism, church leaders of the resistance turned to their sixteenth-century roots in Luther and the Lutheran Confessions.[40] An example of this recovery of the tradition is Hans Christoph von Hase's study of the Magdeburg Confession as a "case of Confession" in the face

38. Peter F. Drucker, *The End of Economic Man: The Origins of Totalitarianism* (New York: John Day, 1939; repr., London: Transaction, 2009).

39. There is not space here to discuss Luther's crucial theological contributions of the two kingdoms and the estates. For an analysis of the legal and social significance of Luther's turning "the traditional theory of spiritual and temporal authority on its side," see John Witte Jr., *Law and Protestantism: The Legal Teachings of the Lutheran Reformation* (Cambridge: Cambridge University Press, 2002). For an extensive discussion of Luther's social ethics in relation to war, see Gerta Scharffenorth, *Den Glauben ins Leben ziehen ... Studien zu Luthers Theologie* (Munich: Kaiser, 1982), esp. 205–312.

40. Among the many examples is the series of some fifty pamphlets under the general heading *Bekennende Kirche* by Kaiser publishing house in Munich from 1933 to 1937, when the publisher was closed by the Nazi state. The series was initially edited by the Munich pastor Christian Stoll along with Theodor Ellwein, and included authors such as Martin Niemöller. The stated purpose of the series was to disseminate the discussions and studies of the Confessing Church in Bavaria in light of Luther's theology and the Lutheran Confessions.

of political oppression.[41] Von Hase's study of sixteenth-century Lutheran resistance was an influence on his cousin and confidante Dietrich Bonhoeffer, whose "early resistance writings are steeped in Lutheran resistance resources."[42] Bonhoeffer was not alone in drawing on Luther; another example is the church historian Gerhard Ritter, who participated in the resistance circle in Freiburg.[43]

These brief historical references do not in themselves provide an explicit path for traversing current and future sociopolitical issues and crises, but they do remind us that our tradition may provide valuable insights for the churches' navigation in troubled waters. For example, the emphasis that salvation is received freely from God alone clearly affirms that the gospel needs no political support and that the kingdom of God is not achievable through sociopolitical programs of either the left or the right. As Luther noted, God's kingdom comes on its own without our prayer.[44] The proclamation that salvation is received, not achieved, that justification is by grace alone, plays a critical role in the de-ideologizing of politics; politics is not redemptive and the Bible is not a blueprint for the great society.

Thus Luther rejected all "crusades" in service of utopian dreams and their concomitant nightmares. This is a timely reminder to us in light of the American ideology of spreading "democracy" no matter the cost in blood and treasure. Luther rejected the medieval *corpus Christianum* mentality—the mentality that there is such a thing as a "Christian" society—the mentality that so easily "baptizes" social, political, and ecclesiastical campaigns. Luther's rejection of a crusading mentality is all the more remarkable because his society felt more threatened by Islamic jihad than ours does. In Luther's time, the European conflict with Turkish Muslims raised apocalyptic fears.[45]

41. Hans Christoph von Hase, *Die Gestalt der Kirche Luthers: Der* casus confessionis *im Kampf des Matthias Flacius gegen das Interim von 1548* (Göttingen: Vandenhoeck & Ruprecht, 1940). In his introduction, von Hase expressed his hope that his study of resistance would strengthen the contemporary church. A briefer study on the same topic appeared in 1935: Christian Stoll, *Interim!*, Bekennende Kirche 36 (Munich: Kaiser, 1935).

42. DeJong, *Bonhoeffer's Reception of Luther*, 219; see also chap. 6: "Lutheran Resistance Resources," 183–202.

43. *In der Stunde Null: Die Denkschrift des Freiburger "Bonhoeffer Kreises,"* introduction by Helmut Thielicke, foreword by Gerhart Ritter (Tübingen: Mohr, 1979); Ritter, for many years editor of the *Archiv für Reformationsgeschichte*, also wrote a comprehensive study of the resistance movement: *Carl Goerdeler und die Deutsche Widerstandsbewegung* (Stuttgart: Deutsche Verlags-Anstalt, 1954). See also Hans Maier, ed., *Die Freiburger Kreise: Akademischer Widerstand und Soziale Marktwirtschaft* (Paderborn: Schöningh, 2014). I am grateful to Dr. Mick Grzonka for alerting me to the Freiburg circle and its *Denkschrift*.

44. BC 356–57, 446–49.

45. See Gregory J. Miller, *The Turks and Islam in Reformation Germany* (New York: Routledge, 2018).

To a large degree, the Turkish threat was so terrifying because many Germans understood the conflict between the Hapsburg and Ottoman Empires to be a struggle not between two political powers but between the forces of Christendom and that of its archenemy, Islam.[46]

In 1526, Sultan Suleiman the Magnificent destroyed the Hungarian army and nobility at the battle of Mohacs and placed much of Hungary under Ottoman rule. Then in 1529, he again moved against central Europe in a campaign that ended with the siege of Vienna. This context highlights Luther's rejection of a Christian crusade against the Turks as well as his call for national repentance and self-examination.

> Luther asserts that, as with the people of Nineveh (Jonah 3:6–10), only repentance can still God's chastening rod. But "the big wheels" in the church who would preach a crusade against the Turks "want to fight, not against iniquities, but against the lash of iniquity and thus they would oppose God who says that through the lash he himself punishes us for our iniquities because we do not punish ourselves for them."[47]

Imagine how such a stance would have been received in America right after 9/11!

> Luther's denunciation of the crusade was an important historical contribution to the development of Christian responses to Islam. . . . Luther's opposition to the crusade became embedded in early Protestantism and should be regarded as an important contribution and development in the period. . . . No crusade or holy war was permissible. This represents a significant point of departure from the mainstream of medieval theology,[48]

not to mention our own. One of Luther's greatest achievements was his recognition that the call to legitimate struggle against the Turkish threat was *not* to be equated with a conflict between Islam and Christianity.[49]

Luther's suspicion of government in general included a profound

---

46. Gregory J. Miller, "Luther on the Turks and Islam," in *Harvesting Martin Luther's Reflections on Theology, Ethics, and the Church*, ed. Timothy L. Wengert (Grand Rapids: Eerdmans, 2004), 185–203, 185.

47. Robert Smith, "Luther, the Turks, and Islam," *Currents in Theology and Mission* 34, no. 5 (2007): 351–64, 353; cf. Martin Luther, "On War Against the Turk," LW 46:171: "This fight must be begun with repentance."

48. Gregory J. Miller, "Fighting Like a Christian: The Ottoman Advance and the Development of Luther's Doctrine of Just War," in *Caritas et Reformatio*, ed. David Whitford (St. Louis: Concordia, 2002), 41–57, 48, 50.

49. Johannes Ehmann, "Türken und Islam—Luthers theologische Unterscheidung: Überlegungen zu ihrer Aktualität," *Luther* 2 (2007): 89–94, 91.

suspicion of war. While never a pacifist,[50] Luther opposed war on the basis that it is always the innocent who suffer the most. He consistently held this position against armed conflict from the Wittenberg unrest of 1521–22 through the Knights' Revolt of 1523 and the Peasants' War of 1524–25. In "Whether Soldiers, Too, Can Be Saved" (1526) Luther wrote: "At the very outset I want to say that whoever starts a war is in the wrong."[51] And in his "Commentary on the Sermon on the Mount" (1521), he asserted:

> anyone who claims to be a Christian and a child of God, not only does not start war or unrest; but he also gives help and counsel on the side of peace wherever he can, even though there may have been a just and adequate cause of going to war.[52]

In his 1530 "Commentary on Psalm 82," Luther wrote:

> One must not begin a war or work for it; it comes unbidden all too soon. One must keep peace as long as one can, even though one must buy it with all the money that would be spent on the war or won by the war. Victory never makes up for what is lost by war.[53]

Even if a prince is fulfilling his office to defend his people and is convinced he has a good cause, Luther asserts:

> You ought not to think that justifies anything you do and plunge headlong into battle. It is indeed true that you have a really good reason to go to war and to defend yourself, but that does not give you God's guarantee that you will win.[54]

These are salutary comments in light of our interminable overt and covert wars around the world and our nuclear saber-rattling.

Luther's profound suspicion of rulers—"a prince is a rare bird in heaven"[55]—was matched by an equally profound suspicion of "Mr. Everyman," for, as Luther was fond of saying, "the world wants to be deceived." "Fake news" is not a modern invention. In other words, in politics as in theology, we ignore the depth and pervasiveness of sin at

---

50. See Siegfried Raeder, "Luther und die Türken," in *Luther Handbuch*, Albrecht Beutel (Tübingen: Mohr Siebeck, 2005), 224–31, 226.

51. LW 46:118.

52. LW 21:40.

53. LW 13:57.

54. LW 46:123.

55. LW 21:345; LW 13:212; LW 45:113, 120; LW 46:122; LW 68:275. Günter Brakelmann, *Luther: Ethik des Politischen* (Bielefeld: Luther-Verlag, 2014), 85–87, lists some seventy of Luther's pejorative terms for rulers and then asks if one can say Luther is a toady of the princes.

our peril. When secular authority cloaks war and injustice with appeals
to civil religion, that is, with the misuse of God's name, "we must offer
resistance."[56] "What am I to do now if I live among such spiritual and
secular tyrants? You should not obey them."[57] Christians are called to
resist.

> For God the Almighty has made our rulers mad; they actually think they can
> do—and order their subjects to do—whatever they please. And the subjects
> make the mistake of believing that they, in turn, are bound to obey their
> rulers in everything.[58]

In his 1539 *Zirkulardisputation*, Luther stated that rulers who act outside
their constituted office are "monsters," "raving demons, "lawless tyrants,"
and "bear-wolves"—what we today call totalitarians. Passive resistance
through civil courage is no longer enough; tyrants have to be removed
by any means. This view will later serve as theological justification for
the attempt to remove Hitler.[59]

> St. Peter says in Acts 4[5:29], "We must obey God rather than men."
> Thereby, he clearly sets a limit to the temporal authority, for if we had to do
> everything that the temporal authority wanted there would have been no
> point in saying, "We must obey God rather than men."[60]

Luther himself became the example of such civil disobedience at the Diet
of Worms in 1521.

That Luther's theological exposition of the duty of political resistance
to unjust government is not merely of historical interest may be seen
in its use in the Norwegian and German resistance to Nazism. Eivand
Berggrav (1884–1959), bishop of Oslo under house arrest in the 1940s,
smuggled to his underground pastors his essay "When the Driver Is
Out of His Mind: Luther on the Duty of Disobedience."[61] Berggrav
attributed to Luther the phrase "If the coachdriver is drunk we have to
put a spoke in the wheel." Bonhoeffer used the phrase in his essay "The

---

56. LW 44:49–51.
57. LW 68:276.
58. LW 45:83.
59. Martin Luther, *Die Zirkulardisputation über das Recht des Widerstands gegen den Kaiser.
Matt. 19,21*, WA 39/2:34–89. See Karl Dietrich Erdmann, "Luther über Obrigkeit, Gehorsam
und Widerstand," in *Luther und die Folgen. Beiträge zur sozialgeschichtlichen Bedeutung der
lutherischen Reformation*, ed. Hartmut Löwe and Claus-Jürgen Roepke (Munich: Kaiser, 1983),
29–59.
60. LW 45:111.
61. In Eivand Berggraf, *Man and State*, trans. George Aus (Philadelphia: Muhlenberg, 1951),
300–319.

Church and the Jewish Question." There he discussed possible church responses to an unjust state:

> The third possibility is not just to bandage the victims under the wheel, but to put a spoke in the wheel itself. Such action would be direct political action, and is only possible and required when the church sees the state fail in its function of creating law [justice] and order.[62]

Indirect political action is also an option. It worked effectively in the former East Germany, where the Lutheran churches provided haven for political discussion and eroded Communist power through services of preaching, prayer, and music. The church's emphasis on the "fearlessness of truth" and nonviolent demonstrations played a significant role in the 1989 demise of the East German Communist rule.[63]

POLITICS IN THE PULPIT

Luther understood himself as a pastor and theologian, not as a politician, but this in no way minimized or limited his pastoral and theological concern for the secular realm of political decisions and involvement. He viewed political decisions as an essential component of the commission to proclaim the gospel to the world and to emphasize to persons in positions of authority their obligations and responsibilities to their neighbors. Luther understood every political problem as a religious challenge that must be investigated in terms of its expression of the will of God.

For Luther, the religious challenge of political problems was to be addressed in the pulpit. The role of the preaching office, in addition to proclaiming the gospel, Luther argued, is to preach God's law to unmask hidden evils, so they may be addressed by the state. Luther epitomized what is known as "frank speech." He did not hesitate to apply his "apocalyptic strategy of exposure by confrontation" in the pulpit as well as in tracts. For Luther a function of preaching is, in the words of Heiko Oberman, "to unmask *hidden* injustice, thus saving the souls of duped Christians and opening the eyes of the secular authorities for their

62. Dietrich Bonhoeffer, "The Church and the Jewish Question," in *Dietrich Bonhoeffer: Witness to Jesus Christ*, John de Gruchy (London: Collins, 1988), 124–30, 127. See also Ulrich Duchrow, *Global Economy: A Confessional Issue for the Churches?* (Geneva: WCC Publications, 1987), chap. 3: "What to Do if the Driver Is Drunk: The Answer of Luther and Bonhoeffer."

63. See Helmar Junghans, "The Christians' Contribution to the Non-violent Revolution in the German Democratic Republic in the Fall of 1989," in *Martin Luther in Two Centuries* (St. Paul: Lutheran Brotherhood Foundation Reformtion Library, Luther Seminary, 1992), 86–99.

mandate to establish *civil* justice."[64] As Doug Marlette, the late Pulitzer Prize–winning editorial cartoonist for the *Atlanta Constitution*, noted, free expression is important for a healthy society. All leaders are aware that information is power. If you can control the information, you can control the people.[65] A similar point is attributed to George Orwell: "In times of deceit, telling the truth can be a revolutionary act."[66] In a 1529 sermon on Jesus before Pilate, Luther stated:

> Christ has shown and taught us that one should not keep silence about the truth before powerful men and lords, but should rather admonish and rebuke them for their injustice. . . . A Christian should bear witness to the truth and die for the sake of the truth. If, then, he is to die for the sake of the truth, he must confess the truth with his lips and rebuke the lie.[67]

Hence the Latin text of the Augsburg Confession begins with the reference to Psalm 119:46: "I will also speak of your decrees before kings, and shall not be put to shame."[68]

The "unmasking" of injustice and "opening the eyes of secular authorities" is not done in a corner but in the preaching office "in the congregation . . . openly and boldly before God and men."[69] It is God's will, Luther continued, "that those who are in the office [of ministry] and are called to do so shall rebuke and judge their gods [i.e., the princes] boldly and openly."[70]

> To rebuke rulers is not seditious, provided it is done . . . by the office to which God has committed that duty, and through God's Word, spoken publicly, boldly, and honestly. To rebuke rulers in this way is, on the contrary, a praiseworthy, noble, and rare virtue, and a particularly great service to God, as the psalm [Psalm 82] here proves. It would be far more seditious if a preacher did not rebuke the sins of rulers; for then he makes people angry and sullen, strengthens the wickedness of the tyrants, becomes a partaker in it, and bears responsibility for it.[71]

> For a preacher is neither a courtier nor a hired hand. He is God's servant and slave, and his commission is over lords and slaves; as the psalm says: "He judges and rebukes the gods." . . . He is to do what is right and proper, not

64. Heiko A. Oberman, "Teufelsdreck: Eschatology and Scatology in the 'Old' Luther," in *The Impact of the Reformation* (Grand Rapids: Eerdmans, 1994), 62.

65. Doug Marlette, *Shred This Book!* (Atlanta: Peachtree, 1988), 156.

66. I am grateful to Dr. Cynthia Moe-Lobeda for this quote.

67. LW 69:236–37.

68. BC 31; LW 49:353–56.

69. LW 13:49.

70. LW 13:50.

71. LW 13:50.

with a view to favor or disfavor, but according to law, that is, according to God's Word, which knows no distinction or respect of persons.[72]

But as Luther noted in a sermon on Jesus cleansing the temple, the civil authorities want to control the pulpit in order to hear only what they want.[73]

Luther's orientation for our public witness is that Christians are called to responsible service *in* the world, politically and militarily as well as other ways, for the sake of the well-being of others. Our responsible service is rooted in the gospel's unequivocal promise that our destiny with God is God's own free gift and is not contingent on our works. Since our certainty of redemption derives not from what we do but rather from what God has done, we are emancipated

- *from* all forms of political ideology that equate the kingdom of God with particular political and military programs that "baptize" our way of life and depict our enemies as the children of darkness—or in more recent phrases, "evil empires," the "axis of evil," or Islam—and us as the children of light; and

- *for* the consolation of the gospel, which not only encourages us to assume public responsibilities but also comforts our consciences and those of our leaders in the midst of the ambiguities inherent in choices made in a fallen world.

Prophetic proclamation of the gospel exposes our own sin, even in our good works, and opens our eyes to our own contributions to creation's groaning and travail. In its own way God's judgment also emancipates us

- *from* the illusion that any political and military decision or action may be unambiguous and righteous; and

- *for* political and military decisions and actions without the self-deception and the self-righteousness that Christians *as Christians* have any special expertise on peace and just war above and beyond that available to anyone of reason and goodwill.

---

72. LW 13:51.

73. "Those worldly lords want to rule over the spiritual kingdom and to control the pulpit and church so that I shall have to preach what you, Count, want to hear! No, I would sooner let the devil take my place and preach." Martin Luther, *Saemmtliche Werke* (Erlangen: Verlag Carl Heyder, 1826–1857), 46, 186, cited in Berggrav, *Man and State*, 310. Cf. WA 46:737,2–4).

Such prophetic preaching reminds us that God's law, summarized in the Ten Commandments as a kind of human survival kit, works to restrain evil and promote the common good. God's law, known through reason, is operative everywhere in the world in one form or another as the principle of order. This universality of the law emancipates us

- *from* requiring agreement in doctrine, be it theological or political, before cooperation toward achieving limited objectives beneficial to all parties;

- *for* negotiation for the common good on the basis of mutual self-interest because our concern is national and international well-being, not our own moral purity; and

- *for* the critical use of reason to achieve the political goal of earthly welfare.

These abstractions of the resources of our Lutheran tradition reflect the theme of Christian freedom. This theme—so eloquently expressed by Luther's dictum that the Christian is at one and the same time a perfectly free lord of all, subject to no one, and a perfectly dutiful servant of everyone, subject to everyone[74]—is a timely orientation in the face of the utopian paths and dystopian chasms surrounding the issues of peace and war in the nuclear age. Christian freedom liberates us both from the illusion that the next technological breakthrough will save us and the despair that nuclear holocaust is just around the corner.[75]

The Christian is to take seriously the task of world-building and the maintenance of culture, society, and civilization, but always with the conviction that every culture, every system of justice, and every political-economic structure is only relative and instrumental for the humanization of people. Tradition is to be conserved with awareness of its dehumanizing aspects and its penultimacy. Reason and love are to be active in the continual task of promoting the common good in the recognition that God—not the past, not the state, not the economy, not "our way of life," not even the church—is sovereign in history. For Luther, faith alone grants the security to live within the human insecurity of relative social and political structures. It is only by faith that persons can avoid the defensive sanctification of past, present, or future

74. LW 31:344.

75. See my introduction to *Peace and the Just War Tradition*, ed. Michael J. Stelmachowicz (St. Louis: Concordia, 1986); and Viggo Mortensen, ed., *Krieg, Konfession, Konziliarität: Was heist "gerechter Krieg" in CA XVI heute?/War, Confession and Conciliarity: What Does "Just War" in the Augsburg Confession Mean Today?* (Hannover: Lutherisches Verlagshaus, 1993).

goods and values. Faith is the enabling ground of the person who is content to be human and to let God be God.

In one of his sermons, Luther reminded his congregation that we are guests in this world. Our lives are transitory.

> But since it is God's will that everyone should serve his fellows here . . . we will do whatever is enjoined upon us. We will serve . . . so long as we can; we would not relax our service even if we knew we had to depart this very hour and leave all earthly things. For, God be praised, had we to die now we would know where we belong, where our home is. While we are here, however, on the way, it is ours to fulfill the obligations of our earthly citizenship.[76]

It is this faith that led in the wake of the disaster and despair of World War II to the saying often attributed to Luther: "Even if I knew the world would end tomorrow, I would still plant an apple tree today."[77]

---

76. WA 21:342–43; cf. LW 77:196–99.

77. Martin Schloemann, *Luthers Apfelbäumchen? Ein Kapital deutscher Mentalitätsgeschichte seit dem Zweiten Weltkrieg* (Göttingen: Vandenhoeck & Ruprecht, 1994).

2.

Lutheran Faith: Rebellion and Responsibility

KIRSI I. STJERNA

Followers of the Lutheran theological heritage value freedom.[1] This core value speaks of Luther's fundamental theological insight, drawn from the Scriptures, about the existential freedom found in grace-based living and the equality and justice it offers for human relations. The ultra-Lutheran expression "justification by faith" addresses freedom on the fundamental level of human existence: freedom from regrets, freedom for new beginnings. It speaks of spiritual freedom that is not apart from political freedoms. The English words *justification* and *justice* communicate the integral connection between the individual experience of being freed by grace and the communal responsibilities to ensure freedoms for others. Lutheran theology underscores freedom as a divine gift and a right of every human being. Lutheran Christian identity involves intentionally expressing this radical love in different aspects of human relations and, when necessary, standing against the antifreedom powers and structures in our world.[2] Lutheran witness calls for a vocal presence—even faithful rebellion—in the affairs of our world.

Freedom is a key Lutheran word and one that can renew our focus when assessing the Lutheran story of the past and its significance for us in discerning direction for today from a particularly Lutheran theological

---

1. The angle and the topic of this essay arise from, first, my shared research with my spouse-partner Brooks Schramm on Luther and the Jews; second, my personal and professional interests as a Lutheran pastor and a seminary professor constantly deliberating on the value and credibility of Lutheran theology today and my responsibility to "reform" Lutheran theological language from such tarnished connections as anti-Semitism; and third, the alarming political developments in our world, in the United States more specifically but also beyond, as the crimes of anti-Semitism are on the rise, again.

2. The word "world" refers to our shared life in the universe and society, with all that entails, including political structures, with no negative association, as in "world" vs. "spiritual realm."

standpoint. Other related key words—rising straight out of Lutheran history—are *confessing*, *rebellion*, and *transformation.*

LUTHER'S FREEDOM AND MODEL OF CONFESSING

Luther's confessing acts and theologically rebellious moves early on in his career made him a reformer. In 1517, Luther drew attention to the areas in religious life where the proclamation and realization of the gospel were faltering, in his observation. People were hungry, physically and spiritually. The suffering people were hoping to find security in wrong or problematic sources, such as the purchase of indulgences. At the same time, the people's already meager resources were heavily taxed by the religious revenue system in which money flowed to Rome and other places far removed from everyday Germans' lives. Didn't the head of the church care, Luther wondered. Did he not know what was happening as if with his blessing, and in Christ's name?

In 1516, Luther had already poked at the theory of salvation and the scholastic theology that provided the normative understanding of grace and its distribution. But it was his Ninety-Five Theses that reached the world with a somewhat ambiguous and subtle form of rebellion and resonated in the hearts of people wondering "what's up?" with the church, the pope, the clergy, and the whole business of religion. Posting the Ninety-Five Theses stands out as an incredibly brave move, not just because of their primary message and content, but for the way Luther stuck his neck stuck out when he sent his text to men in high places—in case they missed the public posting.

Soon after, having been condemned at a public debate (1518) and on the eve of being expelled from the church he loved and had given his whole life for (1521), Luther launched a major program of reforms. His goal was to reach all parts of the church and society, and to call everyone to action—to protect the gospel that was to lift up human lives, rather than serve as an instrument for abuse or an excuse for neglect. In his *Address to the German Nobility* (1520), Luther called the rulers to rise and rescue the gospel from the hands of the papacy (among other things) and articulated several urgent requirements (such as schooling for children and welfare for those in need).

Just a few months later, Professor Luther expanded his criticism of the church's dominant sacramental theology and practice in his treatise *On the Babylonian Captivity of the Church* (1520), ridiculing and suggesting abolishment of many practices that shaped the religious lives of clergy and laity. While he was at it, he bellowed a strong defense of the right for all to marry[3] and made an effort to define the limits of the church's authority, especially when the church appeared to interfere with people's rights and freedom. Finally, he connected with men and women in different walks of life through his manifesto *On Freedom of a Christian* about the limits and responsibilities of being a Christian.[4] The prolific author with a prophetic voice was, not surprisingly, declared an outlaw by the pope in January 1521, and from there the story of Lutherans began. This is the Luther who deserves ongoing attention, and not just every five hundred years. This is a model of feistiness Lutherans can be proud of—and challenged with.

LUTHER AND RADICAL ENGAGEMENT

We have heard the story of Luther's theologically stimulated rebellion so often that we may have become numb to how radical it was: a lonely monk-preacher-professor challenging the entire spiritual empire and, even if unwillingly, gaining a political voice. He was told to be quiet and take back his teachings. He listened to his conscience and spoke not less but more. He was threatened, punished, outlawed, excommunicated. Still he did not stop, not until his last breath. It is worth nothing that Luther acted at great personal risk when he saw that the church was failing to do what it was supposed to do. Yet Luther was no superman, no better person than you or I. He had no great earthly powers or authority. Where did he get his motivation, or chutzpah, then?

We can discern his sources of power. First, he drew on the Scriptures and the transformative Word of law and gospel that was not, in his view, properly proclaimed, experienced, or realized; the Word made him squirm and feel acutely aware of his surroundings. Second, he witnessed human issues around him, combined with the existential angst he felt personally. Reading his Ninety-Five Theses, we can sense his resolution: something had to be said and done about a whole lot of issues. Luther had not figured out exactly what and how and with what consequences, but he acted anyway, feeling compelled to do so. Identifying some issues as urgent, he felt that addressing them was a matter both of integrity and

3. See Kirsi I. Stjerna, "On Marriage, with Luther, for Gay and Straight," *Seminary Ridge Review* 16, no. 2 (2014): 64–85; also published as "Luther on Marriage: Considerations in Light of Contemporary Concerns," in *Glaube und Denken: Theologie im Spannungsfeld von Kirche und Politik; Hans Schwarz zum 75 / Theology in Engagement with Church and Politics: Hans Schwarz on the Occasion of His 75th Birthday*, ed. Matthias Heesch, Thomas Kothmann, and Craig Nessan (Frankfurt am Main: Peter Lang, 2015), 409–26.

4. Revised or new translations of these texts are available in the new six-volume series *The Annotated Luther* (Minneapolis: Fortress Press, 2015–2017); see particularly vol. 1, *The Roots for Reform*, ed. Timothy Wengert (Minneapolis: Fortress Press, 2015).

of his identity as a Christian. There are times to stand up or stick one's neck out for the sake of the truth expressed in the Scriptures and in the face of acute human needs.

We could ask ourselves, What would stoke up Luther today, and what level of resistance would he be willing to offer? It is safe to assume Luther would use social media and any other channels available to mobilize Christians to act on problems needing attention. He would not stay home, safe and unengaged.

While contemplating Luther's epic example of theologically grounded resistance and the power of his freedom theology, Lutherans today can benefit from taking a look at the more recent past and seeing how Lutherans have since engaged the world—for better or worse. Two examples come from relatively recent German history: the Berlin Wall and the Holocaust.

Why these? As we read the news today—riots in Charlottesville and other senseless shootings and acts of terror around the country, recurring anti-Semitic acts of terror, tensions between ordinary people and government officials in the United States, fragile global politics and widespread suffering—we hear eerie echoes of events from not that long ago. We remember when significant evil happened, in full public view and with "normal" people's involvement, when Lutherans' action/inaction, resistance/complicity mattered a great deal. If we do anything with history, we should, by golly, learn from it!

In 1989, a miracle of a sort happened, when the notorious Berlin Wall, which separated the free people in the West and their not-so-free neighbors in the East, came crumbling down, piece by piece. It was destroyed by the people whose lives it had been limiting and endangering for nearly three decades. A lesser-known aspect of the story is that the peaceful protest moment began in a Lutheran gathering for "prayer and politics" in Leipzig.

Faithfully assembling for worship, lingering after service for prayer and mutual support, and meeting again on Mondays, sometimes with only a few people present, to talk about things that matter, Lutheran worshipers created the space for the largest peaceful demonstration in German history to occur. After nearly a decade of small meetings, on the evening of October 9, 1989, eight thousand people flocked to the church, and between seventy thousand and one hundred thousand joined for a candle-lit walk through the city, in resistance to Communist tyranny and standing bravely for freedom at the risk of personal injury and imprisonment. The police "joined" the walk by not shooting a single shot. This walk of ordinary people (and other less publicized freedom acts) occurred in the *Heldenstadt* (City of Heroes), as Leipzig became called, and led to the tearing down of the Berlin Wall.

This incredible piece of history stands as one of the laudable examples of Christians witnessing with integrity and courage and concretely changing the world, moving toward freedom for all. In this story, we see the spiritual and the political intertwined in a positive way; we see how faith can fuel changes in society, how it can take actual walls down. The Leipzig events are a witness to the fact that the gospel of transformation and freedom—what Luther proclaimed—has real legs in the real world, that is, human legs, when people are moved to "do" something. Who knew that walking through the streets while holding candles would become such a stimulus for a radical change! Ordinary people made a difference, as "confessing" Christians, Lutherans, on the frontlines.[5]

For every victorious story, though, there is a tragedy. In a category of its own stands Lutheran Christians' active or passive association with the Nazi power in World War II Germany. A painful example from recent history involves those confessing the Christian faith, many affiliated with its Lutheran expression, while failing to resist the powers of the time who committed unspeakable crimes against humanity on a grand scale, under the gaze of "normal," law-abiding citizens.

With the rise of Adolf Hitler to power in Germany, a pseudo-scientific ideology claiming the superiority of the Aryan race[6] was promoted. To ensure the so-called purity of the supposedly superior Germanic race, methods were designed to exterminate those considered a threat to the German people and heritage or thought to be unworthy of living, such as the Roma people, homosexuals, political activists, the developmentally challenged, and, most of all, the Jews.[7] In the last case, the word *racism*[8] is most appropriate to describe the Nazi ideology's roots and orientation.[9]

---

5. See Andrew Curry, "A Peaceful Revolution," *Spiegel Online International*, October 9, 2009, https://tinyurl.com/y8mfjonc.

6. See United States Holocaust Memorial Museum, "Nazi Racism," *The Holocaust Encyclopedia*, https://tinyurl.com /y99te8ac.

7. See United States Holocaust Memorial Museum, "Final Solution," *The Holocaust Encyclopedia*, https://tinyurl.com/y8hkl7oq.

8. Anti-Semitism, hatred of the Jews and Jewish faith in particular, was an essential ingredient in the hate speech and killing acts engaged in by the Nazis. Anti-Semitism has to do with Jews as people, as an ethnic group, but also as persons practicing Jewish faith. See, e.g., United States Holocaust Memorial Museum, "Antisemitism," *The Holocaust Encyclopedia*, https://tinyurl.com/y9u3z6yo.

9. I use the word consciously, because Jews were portrayed and objectified with particular physical characteristics and as an ethnic group, as well as a religious group, and because systematized discrimination against them echoes the expressions of racism in the United States, especially toward black people. Living post–Martin Luther King Jr. and the civil rights movement, Christians are called to name racism where it is expressed, in any shape or form. Jew-hatred is a form of that racism.

A most outrageous crime against humanity ensued with the terrifyingly effective, politically sanctioned, precisely organized execution of people in death camps. Hitler's "Final Solution" aimed to erase the Jews from Europe. The Jews were named the number-one enemy of the German nation, "the parasites." This view was effectively disseminated through propaganda, the poison that finds its way into daily jokes and fuels implicit biases. While the Nazi crimes against humanity targeted different groups, the killing of six million Jews specifically demonstrates the breakdown of humanity.[10]

"Some of them were neighbors." That was the title of a special exhibit at the United States Holocaust Memorial Museum in 2017.[11] From picture after picture, story after story, visitors to the exhibit could learn who the perpetrators, the active or the silent partners, were. Neighbors. Normal human beings, with names and addresses, pets and children. No evil people with horns, just people capable of great evil. This is what Hannah Arendt calls the "banality of evil."[12]

In addition to the killing of human beings and the torture and humiliation imposed on fellow humans by the Nazis in the camps, another side to the story underscores the depth of the breakdown of humanity: all of that horror happened under the eyes of "ordinary" Christians, who were minding their own business, involved somehow in their jobs, or afraid of getting in trouble themselves, or who knowingly or subconsciously embodied the centuries-old Christian sense of superiority over their Jewish neighbors.

Surely there were exceptions. Most famously, Dietrich Bonhoeffer, a Lutheran theologian, pastor, and author went to his death resisting the Nazi ideology, having plotted Hitler's assassination and actively called for resistance on theological grounds. Similarly, Sophie Scholl, a young student in Munich, raised in a Lutheran home and drawn to the study of religion, went to her death due to her brave involvement with the "White Rose," a peaceful resistance movement organized by young students against "all things Nazi" and for human freedom.[13]

Another exception to the complicity was the Barmen Confession of

---

10. See Holocaust Memorial Museum, "Final Solution."

11. The museum's educational resources are rich, thoroughly researched, and easily available via the internet.

12. See Hannah Arendt, *Eichmann in Jerusalem: A Report on the Banality of Evil* (New York: Penguin Classics, 2006).

13. See Eberhard Bethge, *Dietrich Bonhoeffer: A Biography*, trans. Victoria J. Barnett (Minneapolis: Fortress Press, 2000). Hans Scholl and Sophie Scholl, *At the Heart of the White Rose: Letters and Diaries of Hans and Sophie Scholl*, ed. Inge Jens (Walden, NY: Plough, 2017). Sophie and her brother Hans were executed on February 22, 1943, with their friends Willi Graf, Christoph Probst, and Alexander Schmorell.

1934:[14] a group of evangelical theologians joining with the "Pastors' Emergency League" to defend the newly formed Christian Confessing Church. They stood apart from the "German Christians," who subscribed to Nazi ideology, amplified its voice, and more or less actively promoted Nazi politics. The Confessing Church, formed out of desperation and as an act of theological resistance, sought to protect the gospel and the integrity of the Christian church and tried to argue theologically for the necessary separation from the day's politics. The confession does not endorse Christians separating themselves from politics. Quite the contrary, its very founding was a highly political move that speaks with deep conviction of the ramifications of the gospel. As proof of its impact, the Confessing Church had to operate underground, until in 1948 the Protestant churches from different regions were united into the Evangelical Church in Germany.

Apart from these examples, the silent, apparent compliance of the majority of Christians in those days would be hard to ignore. As the concentration camps were liberated, some of these "neighbors" were forced by the American liberators to come and see for themselves the mass graves; the emaciated bodies of men, women, children; the starved and tortured prisoners of the camps—people who were now free, whereas the "observers" would never be free from their compliance and neglect.

In retrospect, we can blame those people for their "sin" of compliance. We can be outraged and ask, "Why did they not do something? Didn't they read the signs and see what was happening, before it was too late?" Yet, if we are honest, most of us would have probably been walking in those Christians' guilty shoes, as well. Most of us would not have had the courage of Sophie Scholl to "do something, do anything" to resist a government about to commit serious crimes against humanity and compromise human freedom.

The good, or the bad, news is that we again live in a time when similar dynamics are in place, and we have individual and collective choices to make about where we stand, what we tolerate—and what is going to upset us enough to "do something, do anything." And perhaps most importantly, as those drinking from the fountains of the Lutheran Christian theology of freedom, the time is upon us to be prophetic and political. We must dare to name sins as sins and to identify sources of hope, not accepting evil as good or necessary, but proclaiming the

14. See "Theological Declaration of Barmen," Internet Sacred Text Archive, https://tinyurl.com/y9s3xhbn (taken from Arthur C. Cochrane, *The Church's Confession under Hitler* [Philadelphia: Westminster Press, 1962], 237–42).

alternative—the message of hope and restoration—and discerning the necessary steps to take and in whose company we will take them.

So, let's name one area that needs our urgent care, one of the insidious evils that we all are aware of: racism. It is a beast that doesn't die, an irrational evil, a sin, embedded in our social, economic, and political structures and imaginations, expressed in public and private aspects of our lives. A particular expression of racism is anti-Semitism, and it is from that angle that I return to Nazi Germany to underscore the particular prophetic and political task for Lutheran Christians today.[15]

ANTI-SEMITISM AND LUTHER

The Nazi ideology had a pseudo-scientific base with its aim of "ethnic cleansing"—a horrifying term in itself and an extreme expression of racism. But racism is not "just" a Nazi crime. Racist crimes against particular ethnic groups with an intent to destroy, that is, genocides, took place before and have happened since World War II. Recent genocides in Myanmar, Bosnia, Rwanda, and Cambodia were preceded by South Africans' struggle with apartheid and the abuse of the Aboriginals in Australia. North Americans are still dealing with the impact of the colonizers' violence against the Natives of the land. In Germany, as in other contexts where genocide has been committed, political, irrational, and terrifying factors were many, but there was also a religious side, which cannot be ignored.[16]

Nazi propagandists knew how to draw from the works of many a Christian teacher to support their mission by explicitly associating it with Christian identity and values. There were many voices to choose from. Unfortunately, Christian history has been built with the contributions of theologians who hold implicitly or explicitly anti-Semitic views—all the way from Paul, Origen of Alexandria, Augustine of Hippo, and John of Chrysostom onward. Nazi appropriation forces Christians—Protestant and Catholics alike—to unfold and reckon with this nasty continuum.[17]

Our dear Martin Luther also wrote explicitly about the Jews with theologically argued aggression, and these writings have been widely and wildly disseminated throughout the world. He was a central

15. A colleague of mine from Berkeley, a Jewish scholar whose parents survived the Holocaust, said recently, "The world is again not safe for a Jew." She said her parents' generation had said, "Give it fifty years," and here we are living in times when anti-Jewish speech again seems permissible.

16. See United States Holocaust Memorial Museum, "What Is Genocide?," https://tinyurl.com/yay4o4qm.

17. See, e.g., Robert Michael, *Holy Hatred: Christianity, Antisemitism, and the Holocaust* (New York: Palgrave Macmillan, 2006).

Christian figure evoked by Nazi propaganda. Important Luther remembrance dates were used to grab the people's attention and to imply the greatest theological leader of the German people passively supported Nazi agendas. Most notoriously, the Kristallnacht of November 9–10, 1938, took place on Luther's birthday.[18] Also, once upon a time, a Nazi flag flew from the balcony of the *Lutherhalle*, Luther's famous home in Wittenberg.

At the United States Holocaust Memorial Museum in Washington, DC,[19] a short film on the history of anti-Semitism includes a section on Martin Luther.[20] The official declaration of remorse from the ELCA to the Jewish community is also displayed at the same museum.[21]

There is much to understand, learn, and think about racism and anti-Semitism and the association of these words with Luther and Lutheran theology today.[22] The more one learns on this topic, the more questions arise and the more support one needs to faithfully profess Christian faith in its Lutheran dialect. What is needed is a reformed grammar that in no uncertain terms disassociates the Lutheran faith from anything that would perpetuate contemporary linkages between Lutheranism and anti-Semitism.[23]

Martin Luther wrote about the Jews and Jewish faith throughout his career. From the earliest sermons and lectures on Psalms (1513) until his last word in a sermon in Eisleben (1546), we could say that the Jews were on his mind.[24] He was obsessed with the concept "Jew" and had

18. See United States Holocaust Memorial Museum, "Kristallnacht," *The Holocaust Encyclopedia*, https://tinyurl.com/y86ybal2.

19. The United States Holocaust Memorial Museum educates a wide population about the dangers of anti-Semitism and genocide, with a respectful remembering of the victims of the Holocaust and critical shedding of light on the facts and the perpetrators.

20. See United States Holocaust Memorial Museum, "Confront Hate and Anti-Semitism," https://tinyurl.com/yavhrprz.

21. *The Declaration of the ELCA to the Jewish Community*, Evangelical Lutheran Church in America, https://tinyurl.com/y8hxl2jo: "On April 18, 1994, the ELCA Churchwide Assembly adopted the 'Declaration,' which repudiates Luther's anti-Jewish writings, expresses deep regret for their historical consequences, and reclaims the desire to live in 'love and respect for Jewish people.'"

22. See, e.g., Brooks Schramm, "Luther and the Jews," in *Martin Luther: A Christian between Reforms and Modernity*, ed. Alberto Melloni (Berlin: de Gruyter, 2017); Stephen G. Burnett, "Jews and Luther/Lutheranism," in *Dictionary of Luther and the Lutheran Traditions*, ed. Timothy J. Wengert et al. (Grand Rapids: Baker Academic, 2017); Christopher Ocker, "Martin Luther and Anti-Judaism and Anti-Semitism," *Oxford Research Encyclopedias*, November 2016, https://tinyurl.com/ybcd66bw; Dorothea Wendebourg, "Martin Luther, Jews, and Judaism," *Oxford Research Encyclopedias*, March 2017, https://tinyurl.com/y7p2tqyy.

23. Brooks Schramm and Kirsi I. Stjerna, eds., *Martin Luther, the Bible, and the Jewish People: A Reader* (Minneapolis: Fortress Press, 2012) is written for this kind of educational purpose. The following observations on Luther and the Jews are based on research presented in this book, which features a comprehensive sampling of Luther's own texts, with introductions.

24. Schramm and Stjerna, *Martin Luther*.

much to say on the topic, although the basis for his knowledge was not exactly reliable. A typical Christian of his time, he mingled with fellow Christians and drew from Christian sources.

When exploring Luther's views on the Jews, scholars have typically listed Luther's last publications as the most important: *On Jews and Their Lies*, *Last Words of David*, and *On the Ineffable Name*, and his last two sermons with a "postlude" titled "Admonition against the Jews" to top it all.[25] These works are deliberately and explicitly anti-Semitic. Luther attacks the Jewish faith, its integrity, and, finally, its purpose.[26] Furthermore, in these works he offers a solution for the ecclesial and political leaders to "deal" with the Jews by either extinguishing their faith or removing them from "Christian" lands and proximity.

Luther's most infamous *Judenratschlag*, "advice" regarding the Jews, comes from his treatise *On Jews and Their Lies*, particularly chilling to read after the rise and fall of Nazism (see table 1).

Table 1

To the Civil Authorities	To Pastors and Preachers
1. Burn down synagogues	1. Burn down synagogues
2. Destroy Jewish homes	2. Confiscate prayer books, Talmudic writings, and the Bible
3. Confiscate prayer books and Talmudic writings	3. Prohibit Jewish prayer and teaching
4. Forbid rabbis to teach	4. Forbid Jews to utter the name of God publicly
5. Abolish safe-conduct for Jews	
6. Prohibit usury to the Jews	
7. Force manual labor on the Jews	

25. The most commonly used *Judenschriften* from Luther with this question are the following: *That Jesus Christ Was Born a Jew* (1523) (LW 45:199–229; TAL 5:391–440; WA 11:314–36); *Against the Sabbatarians* (1538) (LW 47:65–98; WA 50:312–37); *On the Jews and Their Lies* (1543) (LW 47:137–306; TAL 5:441–608; WA 53:417–552); *On the Ineffable Name* (1543) (WA 53: 579–648; TAL 5:609–66); *On the Last Words of David* (1543) (LW 15:265–352; WA 54:28–100); *Admonition against the Jews* (1546) (LW 58).

26. Also, Luther's 1526 commentary on Psalm 109 (LW 14); 1537 letter to Rabbi Josel of Rosheim (Schramm and Stjerna, *Martin Luther*); 1543 lecture on Isaiah 9 (WA 40/3); and 1544 lecture on Isaiah 53 (WA 40/3).

Luther's *On Jews and Their Lies* and the other explicitly anti-Jewish works from his last years are only the tip of the iceberg and a culmination of Luther's career-long deliberation on the "Jewish question." His obsession was, primarily, to refute Jewish faith, and secondarily to "deal" with Jews still practicing their faith and not converting to Christianity, and thereby opposing the very core of Lutheran proclamation of the good news! He also labored to prove the superiority of Christian interpretation of Scripture and to establish Christians' exclusive holding of the truth and right reading of the Scriptures. Luther wanted to prove that Christians are the chosen people of God and have in that regard replaced in God's eyes the Jews who wish not to convert. His entire theological grammar about grace and gift-righteousness essentially involved his argumentation against the Jewish faith and (how he understood) the Jewish meaning of the law.

Luther's reasoning, obviously, does not fare well in our world, where the existence of multiple faiths is acknowledged, interreligious dialogue is normal, and Christians, not to mention Lutherans, hardly have a monopoly on religious matters. We do well to view Luther as a medieval man. Luther was living and breathing the air of late medieval Christianity, in a context where there was no room for alternate views—or facts! (Over the centuries, being a Christian has meant to proclaim an exclusive gospel and prove others wrong, with the word or with a sword.) Most of Luther's contemporaries experienced and imagined their world as fully Christian, one where "others" do not belong, can easily be slandered, and are considered threats, parasites, even nonhuman. This mindset was defended by drawing on basic Christian theological views, and it was enhanced by the reality that Christians did not mingle with Jews in their daily lives. Luther's and his contemporaries' knowledge of Jews and Jewishness was based on an abstraction or a caricature, drawn from ubiquitous slandering humor and propaganda.

In addition to mocking the Jews in printed materials and performing arts, Christian churches prominently displayed blaspheming images against the Jews. An example of such an image is the *Judensau*, prominently featured in Luther's home church, the Marienkirche: a scandalous image of Jewish rabbis examining the rear of a sow and Jewish boys sucking the teats of the same sow. This was a commonplace scene for Christian churchgoers, most of whom would not even bat an eyelash at such "humor." The mockery was enhanced by the very real gap between Jews and Christians in real life. The mocking did not "feel" like it had that much to do with real people.

This kind of objectifying and distancing is dangerous in any context.

In our day, we have become more aware of expressions of racism and hurt via supposedly harmless humor. Some of the concrete chances to eradicate racism in our midst start here. What jokes and comments do we not tolerate? Are we willing to hold each other accountable in this regard? And what steps are we willing to take to get to know our neighbors as they are and where they are? We must also ask the deeper question: What structures in our world facilitate interaction and integration vis-à-vis "the other"—and who is she?

In Luther's time, there were serious limitations on interaction between Jews and Christians. As all kinds of measures kept Christians and Jews separate, the power dynamics favored the Christian majority. While business relations were possible, friendships and intermarriages were discouraged, the latter also forbidden legally. There was no normal sharing of a meal or fellowship that would have offered opportunities for personal knowing of "the other." Christian children were raised to be suspicious of the Jews. The requirement that Jews wear distinguishing clothing—the predecessor of the yellow star used by Nazis—went hand in hand with regulations that kept Jewish communities in separate ghettos.

Money and privilege were issues in Luther's time too. Jews had to obey local laws about what professions and sources of income were allowed for them as a special "tolerated" group. Jews were typically allowed to earn income as itinerant merchants and by lending money with interest, a service they provided for Christians. It also made them a target of envy and accusations that they were getting rich at the expense of Christians' needs.

Luther was vocal in his rejection of so-called usury, moneylending for interest, which Jews practiced. As the banking industry developed, Christians entered the business of moneylending as well, and this was not good news for the Jewish bankers. Just as Jews could pay for protection and (limited) rights—for example, to live, travel, practice a profession in the given area—Christian landowners and business owners with their financial interests in mind could bargain with the local lords for the Jews' expulsion, strip local Jews of their income, and in many ways force them to leave their homes. Use of physical harm, in addition to financial sanctions, was not unheard of.

When violence against Jews occurred, typically a rumor or an accusation was associated with the demand for the Jews to leave. Rumors of Jews engaging in violent acts against Christian children, or blaspheming the eucharistic host—without evidence—could stir up the Christian mob for violent acts. Jews brought to trial on such charges were hardly judged fairly, and while their Christian neighbors, blinded by their superstition and false rumors fueling their fears of the other, exercised what they considered justice on religious grounds, the roots of the charges were more often financial than anything else.

By the order of Christian rulers, Jews were systematically expelled from most European countries from the twelfth century on, and expulsions in the sixteenth-century German-speaking lands were frequent also. Germans were some of the last to receive migrant Jews and refugees, whose paths eventually led toward Eastern European borders. Jews in Luther's world were vulnerable, at the mercy of rulers' protection and permission for travel, work, and residence. As such vulnerable minorities, they posed hardly a threat to Christian individuals and communities—despite Christians' deep-seated fears.

LUTHER, THE JEWS, AND THE BIBLE

Christians have long struggled to understand their identity in relation to Judaism, a religious tradition that existed before the church and gave birth to Christianity. Jesus, born of Mary, was a Jew after all. One of Luther's texts underscores this in the title, *That Jesus Christ Was Born a Jew*. This text, from 1523, made some Jews hope at the time of its publication that Luther was a friend of the Jews—something for which there was a hunger in a world that was tangibly anti-Jewish.[27] That was not his intent, however, and he quickly went on record to make that clear, accusing Jews of misusing his kind words. When he returned to the topic later, he explained that his intent had been to advise Christians to properly prepare Jews for their conversion by embodying Christian love and teaching the Christian faith properly. He was adamantly against forced baptisms, for which he blamed the papal-led Catholic Church, just as he condemned the use of violence. He writes:

> They have dealt with the Jews as if they were dogs rather than human beings; they have done little else than deride them and seize their property. . . . I hope that if one deals in a kindly way with the Jews and instructs them carefully from Holy Scripture, many of them will become genuine Christians and turn again to the faith of their fathers, the prophets and patriarchs.[28]

27. In TAL 5:391–440.
28. TAL 5:402–3. "They have dealt with the Jews as if they were dogs rather than human beings; they have done little else than deride them and seize their property. When they baptize them they show them nothing of Christian doctrine or life, but only subject them to popishness and monkery. When the Jews then see that Judaism has such strong support in Scripture, and that Christianity has become a mere babble without reliance on Scripture, how can they possibly compose themselves and become right good Christians? I have myself heard from pious baptized Jews that if they had not in our day heard the gospel they would have remained Jews

These words give a glimpse at the heart of Luther, the man who cared for his neighbors, as well as a reminder of his unrelenting commitment to ensure that the entire world accept the Christian faith, preferably in the form he was teaching it. It is safe to conclude that at no point in his career would Luther have been open to interreligious dialogue; his goal was conversion to Christianity.

In sorting out Luther's feelings about the Jews, it is helpful to remember that Luther's profession and expertise was the Bible and its interpretation. His special interest was the Hebrew texts, which are sacred for the Jews. Luther had much at stake in reading those texts correctly.

A modern scholar of the Old Testament would naturally seek to learn from multiple sources and interpretations. Not Luther; he was not that modern. The Bible was his sourcebook, his life book. It bothered him deeply that Jews still were reading it, and he dismissed Jewish interpretation of the Scriptures as well as the Jewish practice of faith. He knew Hebrew well enough to consider himself better read than the rabbis, although his self-assessment rather exceeded the reality. In truth, the fierce opponent of the Jews was quite uninformed, while curious, about the practice and foundations of Jewish faith. He knew no practicing Jews in his community, he did not converse with Jewish scholars, and his sources on Judaism were problematic, written by Jewish converts eager to prove the superiority of Christian faith and ensure their own Christian standing.

Looking at the whole of Luther's theological argumentation and his interpretation of the Scriptures, we can conclude two things. First, Luther's biblical interpretation is at the heart of every major argument he makes. Second, Luther in a way needed Jews, so he could make his most important theological point, that grace and salvation were freely given through God's revelation in Christ and in the Word, without works or adherence to the law. Jewish faith, or how he portrayed it, served as the counterpoint to what he had come to see was the true and liberating religion. His personal experience was unfaltering. He "knew." He read

under the cloak of Christianity for the rest of their days. For they acknowledge that they have never yet heard anything about Christ from those who baptized and taught them. I hope that if one deals in a kindly way with the Jews and instructs them carefully from Holy Scripture, many of them will become genuine Christians and turn again to the faith of their fathers, the prophets and patriarchs. They will only be frightened further away from it if their Judaism is so utterly rejected that nothing is allowed to remain, and they are treated only with arrogance and scorn. If the apostles, who also were Jews, had dealt with us Gentiles as we Gentiles deal with the Jews, there would never have been a Christian among the Gentiles. Since they dealt with us Gentiles in such brotherly fashion, we in our turn ought to treat the Jews in a brotherly manner in order that we might convert some of them. For even we ourselves are not yet all very far along, not to speak of having arrived." See Schramm and Stjerna, *Martin Luther*, 89.

the Scriptures with that certainty. He could never, ever understand if anyone else did not have the same experience and certainty.

Luther's views on Judaism in this regard did not change. What did change was the level of his Christian hospitality and patience and what he considered the best tactics for Christians in relation to the Jews. While early on he had dared to hope that some Jews might convert if treated with love and properly taught, Luther finally deemed it best that the Jews be "helped" to find their home elsewhere by stripping from them all the structures that support their faith practice and communities. Out of sight, out of mind, seemed to be his final solution.[29]

This final solution differed from that of the Nazis hundreds year later and was based on different premises, but it is nevertheless an untenable way of thinking—then or today. Yet similar statements about expulsions and walls are heard today in a variety of conversations among Christians. This sad and scary reality alone is a reason for us to dwell with this topic—Luther and the Jews and anti-Semitism.

REJECTING SILENCE AND REPUDIATING THEOLOGICAL ANTI-SEMITISM

Having spent some time reflecting on the problems in Luther's theology, which centers on Christ and condemns the Jews who do not consider Christ as their Messiah, I hope the connections with modern-day sins of racism and anti-Semitism are becoming apparent.

We can name anti-Semitism as a form of racism to be resisted, vocally and consistently. Because Luther's name is in any way associated with anti-Semitism and the racism exercised by Nazis, there must be no tolerance for even a whiff of anti-Semitism, or any other form of racism, in Lutheran company today. Taking the elements of anti-Semitism in Luther's writings and how they have been used means that wherever and whenever we witness acts, gestures, words that speak of or in any way condone anti-Semitism in any form, we are called to resist.

We can also continue to educate ourselves on the dangers of theologically embedded anti-Semitism, starting with Luther, and honestly consider the appropriateness and degrees of hospitality of our

---

29. Luther in 1543, *On the Jews and Their Lies* (TAL 5:572–73): "What shall we Christians do with this rejected and condemned people, the Jews? Since they live among us, we dare not tolerate their conduct, now that we are aware of their lying and reviling and blaspheming. If we do, we become sharers in their lies, cursing, and blasphemy. . . . I shall give you my sincere advice. First, to set fire to their synagogues or schools and to bury and cover with dirt whatever will not burn, so that no man will ever again see a stone or cinder of them. This is to be done in honor of our Lord and of Christendom, so that God might see that we are Christians."

own faith languages, liturgies, proclamation, attitudes, and religious sensitivities. For example, next time we go to worship or lead worship, we could consider, imagine, and reflect on how the language used and the points (typically) made in Christian proclamation may sound to a Jewish person.

With knowledge and self-awareness and critical compassion, we can work, together, toward a shift in orientation in Lutheran hermeneutics in order to proclaim the liberating gospel that shapes the entire Christian faith with integrity and in ways that honor human life and religious expression. And we can accomplish these things without making the Christian grammar of faith normative. There is no simple way to do this, but isn't this what the central Christian message calls everyone to who wants to associate with Jesus of Nazareth?

Where this last point leads us is Christ. As it was for Luther a lifelong journey and a passion, Lutheran Christians' ongoing challenge is to deliberate on these questions: What is the meaning of Christ to us? How shall we walk in the footsteps of Christ and express the core of his message? Compassion and freedom and equality—do these words resonate with how we understand what being a follower of Christ means?

Finally, the issue of anti-Semitism considered as a form of racism raises our awareness of economic injustices that involve all of us on some level. We abhor the events of the past, for example, the ghetto system of the Middle Ages and the Nazi era, and yet today we have ghettos of a sort, all over the United States. We have "designated" areas for different populations. We have gentrification processes in place to benefit those with means at the expense of those in need. In typical American towns, racial segregation is taken as "normal," unspoken but very real. Money matters are typically at the root of this evil, behind which racial biases are obvious and insidious. The job market and opportunities or lack of them in our society reflect racial and economic inequality. These conditions are present in the modern, civilized world. This is to say that in addition to the many theological challenges and opportunities the topic of Luther and the Jews raises, reflection on Luther, anti-Semitism, and racism also invites us to take a new look at our own world and consider, again, what kind of neighbors we are, in our time and our place.

3.

Reclaiming the Empowerment of Ordinary People

MARY JANE HAEMIG

It is often stated that the Reformation lifted the status of ordinary people, but this assertion is rarely fully explored. Usually the focus is on the doctrine of vocation and/or the priesthood of all believers—worthy subjects of reflection, to be sure, but not exhaustive of the ways in which the Reformation affected the lives of ordinary people. Luther and the Wittenberg Reformation sought to empower people—all people, even the forgotten people. They sought to do this through catechizing people in the Christian faith, establishing schools and education for young people, and providing the Bible, worship services, and hymns in the vernacular. This is not an exhaustive list, but it provides a foundation for thinking about the Wittenberg Reformation in relation to the theme of empowerment.

CATECHIZATION

One of the most significant ways the Wittenberg Reformation sought to empower people was through catechizing them in the Christian faith. Please note that for Luther and his fellow Reformers, catechizing (educating in the faith) was for all people—not just young people. Luther complained in his introduction to the Small Catechism (1529) that in his recent experience in the Saxon visitations, "the ordinary person, especially in the villages, knows absolutely nothing about the Christian faith, and unfortunately many pastors are completely unskilled and incompetent teachers."[1] Why did Luther and his fellow Reformers think teaching and learning the catechism important? They wanted to empower all the baptized, producing confident confessors of the Christian faith and thoughtful citizens. A brief review of the reasons they gave for teaching and learning the catechism will help us reflect on how these relate to the theme of empowerment.

The Wittenberg Reformation saw the catechism as a summary of Scripture or introduction to Scripture. In particular, the first three parts of the catechism—Ten Commandments, Apostles' Creed, and Lord's Prayer—summarized Scripture.[2] In his *Little Prayer Book* (1522) Luther commented,

> It was not unintended in God's particular ordering of things that a lowly Christian person who might be unable to read the Bible should nevertheless be obligated to learn and know the Ten Commandments, the Creed, and the Lord's Prayer. Indeed, the total content of Scripture and preaching and everything a Christian needs to know is quite fully and richly comprehended in these three items. They summarize everything with such brevity and clarity that no one can complain or make any excuse that the things necessary for salvation are too complicated or difficult to remember.[3]

Luther thought that these three parts convey the central message of the Bible. The Bible speaks of God's expectations for our lives. The Bible also tells us what God does for us and instructs us in how we communicate with God. The commandments, creed, and Lord's Prayer provide summaries of these. By focusing on the central message—the central plot—the catechism gives readers and listeners an introduction and guide to reading Scripture. Knowing the plot always helps you read the book!

For the Reformers, learning the catechism is never itself an end—either a goal or an endpoint. Luther emphasized in his second series of catechetical sermons that after people have learned the catechism, they should be led further into Scripture.[4] So the catechism was meant to empower people to explore the Bible further. This theme was picked up by later followers of Luther. Lutheran pastor Simon Musaeus (1521 or 1529–76) remarked that people who do not have the catechism to guide them in reading the Bible remain poor and needy in the midst of the great riches of the Bible. He compared them to sick ones who have a

---

1. Preface to the Small Catechism, BC 347.
2. In Luther's first series of catechetical sermons in 1528 he said that in the first three parts of the catechism all Scripture is contained. WA 30/1:2.
3. Martin Luther, *Little Prayer Book* (1522), TAL 4:167; WA 10/2:376.
4. WA 30/1:27.

pharmacy full of healing herbs and spices but cannot use it for lack of proper directions.[5]

The Lutheran Reformers expected the catechism to teach Christians how to read the Bible, making them independent of the whims and caprices of pastors, priests, and false teachers. Notice the assumption is that ordinary people, if given the tools, can understand Scripture.

Second, the Lutheran Reformers saw the catechism as the identifying mark of the Christian. Luther said that those who do not know their catechism should not be counted among Christians. This is really about identity—but a deeper sense of identity than one that merely involved intellectual knowledge. Luther compared the Christian who does not know his catechism to the craftsman who does not know his craft.[6] Just as a craftsman's knowledge defines his very existence, so too knowledge of the catechism defines the life of the Christian. Later Lutheran preachers picked up this theme. Christoph Fischer (1518–69) remarked that no one accepts a tradesman into a guild unless he knows the customs and usages of the trade. So, too, one should not take anyone into the praiseworthy guild of the Christians who does not know the catechism.[7] Musaeus compared Christians who don't know their catechism to cooks who cannot cook.[8]

Notice two things here. First, the identifying mark of the Christian is not a mere ritual (baptism) but rather the faith that baptism produces—a knowledgeable faith that enables one to confess who God is and what God does. Second, notice that the identifying mark of the Christian is not clerical or monastic vows, a particular lifestyle (monastic), or a particular place within an ecclesiastical structure. No, the identifying mark of the Christian is knowledge of how God works and what God does.

Third, the Reformers saw knowledge of the catechism as a weapon in the ongoing fight against sin, the devil, and heretics. They saw the conflicts, temptations, and troubles of ordinary people as important, something to which faith directly speaks. When preaching on the third commandment in 1528, Luther commented: "Since therefore the devil is always soliciting us, it is necessary that we hold the symbol [the Apostles'

---

5. Simon Musaeus, *Catechistisch Examen mit kurtzen Fragen und Antworten / von den aller notwendigsten und wichtigsten Artickeln Christlicher Lere* . . . (Ursel: Nicolaus Henricus, 1568), 6r–v.

6. The Large Catechism, BC 383.

7. Christoph Fischer, *Auslegung der Fu(e)nff Heuptstu(e)cke des Heiligen Catechismi / Gestellet und geprediget durch M. Christofferum Vischer / Hennebergischen Superintendenten / und Pfarherrn zu Meiningen* (Leipzig: Johan Rambaw, 1573), B2r.

8. Musaeus, *Catechistisch Examen*, 5r–v.

Creed] and the Lord's Prayer in our hearts and mouths."[9] In his 1530 preface to the Large Catechism Luther wrote,

> Nothing is so powerfully effective against the devil, the world, the flesh, and all evil thoughts as to occupy one's self with God's Word, to speak about it and meditate upon it. . . . For this reason alone you should gladly read, recite, ponder, and practice the catechism, even if the only advantage and benefit you obtain from it is to drive away the devil and evil thoughts. For he cannot bear to hear God's Word.[10]

The Reformers did not think that the great battles of faith were fought only by the clergy, the hierarchy, or prominent saints in the past. Ordinary Christians needed weapons for use in the ongoing fight against all that could destroy faith and cause the Christian to despair. In the sixteenth century these enemies of the faith were both cosmic (sin, death, and the devil) and temporal (Roman Catholics, Anabaptists, and various Protestant opponents). Importantly, Lutheran preachers wanted to give their listeners hope that these battles would not last forever. Christoph Fischer said that "pious Christians" should not be angry about the controversies but should also "lift up their heads" because their salvation is near. Controversies occur because the devil realizes he does not have much time and therefore is raging most horribly.[11]

Fourth, the Wittenberg Reformers also saw the catechism as a summary of doctrine and as a measure for judging other teaching. Knowing the catechism empowered laypeople to evaluate what they heard—and provided the laity with an important ecclesiastical oversight function. The catechism empowered laity to listen intelligently to sermons and also empowered them to distinguish between true and false teaching, that is, to judge what was being preached and taught to them. This view was revolutionary in its time, both socially and ecclesiastically!

The Reformers wanted intelligent, engaged listeners, not passive acquiescence. One purpose of teaching the catechism was to produce thoughtful hearers of sermons. Fischer told his hearers that the catechism is a sum of, and guide to, the preaching they hear throughout the year.[12] Musaeus stated that the catechism serves hearers "in regard to their own shepherd in this way, that the catechism shows them the right way to understand their sermons." In regard to "strange wolves," the

9. WA 30/1:5.
10. The Large Catechism, BC 381.
11. Fischer, *Auslegung*, 4r.
12. Fischer, *Auslegung*, B1v.

catechism gives to listeners a certain "touchstone and scale to distinguish the damnable lies and many corruptions from the salvific truth."[13]

Some Reformers expanded on how the catechism enables a layperson to recognize and reject false teaching. Johann Gigas (1514–81) in his catechetical sermons engaged in an imaginary dialogue with a parishioner: "Yes, you say, I am a layperson and one teaches this and another that, how can I judge between them?" Gigas responded (in part)

1. In the holy Ten Commandments you have the proper good works that God has commanded through which God is honored and the neighbor is served. For this reason, reject pilgrimages and regulations of food and marriage. . . .

2. In the Apostles' Creed, you hear clearly that Jesus Christ alone your helper and savior is, therefore reject all leaders who point you to the law, to your own or to other's works, to earn heaven.

3. Our Christian faith also declares that Jesus Christ is God's only son and the son of the virgin Mary. . . . The divine and human natures are united in one person. Therefore avoid old and new Nestorians and puffed up chaps who divide the person of Christ, such as Osiander and Stancarus.

4. In your catechism you hear that one should pray in spirit and in truth, that is, in true knowledge of God and in the Name of Jesus Christ. So reject all those who tell you to seek help from dead saints.[14]

Implicit in the above was the assumption that laypeople were aware of theological controversy and could understand theological issues and viewpoints. Laity were assumed to understand not just contemporary issues of practice (such as whether to pray to saints) but also relatively complicated theological issues. Both old controversies—for example, christological controversies—as well as newer controversies—for example, Calvinistic views of the sacraments—were matters laity were expected to understand and to be able to discern the truth about. Learning the catechism became a way that laypersons were empowered to do what previously only a spiritual elite, members of an ecclesiastical hierarchy, had done: to judge what is true and false teaching. Learning

---

13. Simon Musaeus, *Catechismus / Mit kurtzen Fragen unnd Antworten / von den aller notwendigsten und wichtigsten Artickeln Christlicher Lehre / sampt erinnerungen von den fu(o)rnembsten Irrthumen und Corruptelen / durch welche der Teufel jetziger Zeit viel Leute jrre machete und verfu(e)hret / Fu(e)r die kinder und einfeltigen gestellet . . .* (Frankfurt am Main: Nicolaus Bassee, 1580), C1v–C2v.

14. Johann Gigas, *Catechismus Iohannis Gigantis Northusani: Gepredigt zur Schweidnitz . . .* (Franckfurt/Oder: Johan Eichorn, 1578), Bii(v)–Biiii(r).

the catechism gave ordinary people the function of oversight. This upended the hierarchy, in theory if not in practice.

The authority of the layperson to judge all preaching and teaching did not legitimize any judgment that person wanted to make. To the contrary! For the Wittenberg Reformers, this authority was always bound to the Word of God. The catechism was a tool for learning and knowing the Word of God. The Reformers recognized that it is the task of *all* Christians, clergy and lay, to discern what is right and wrong in the faith. All are held accountable to the standards of the apostolic faith, as set forth in Scripture and summarized in creed and confession.

RESPECT FOR ORDINARY PEOPLE

Lutheran catechisms and catechetical sermons from the sixteenth century bear witness to the fact that preachers and teachers assumed that their listeners, even the simplest, could learn and grapple with theological doctrines. They could, for example, learn the distinction between God's work in the law and God's work in the gospel. Catechisms and sermons show that the Reformers wanted to help their listeners reflect on what both these works of God meant for their lives.

Catechisms encouraged people to reflect on God's law. Most Lutheran catechisms of this era, like Luther's Small Catechism, are set up in question-and-answer format. They encouraged not simple recitation of the commandment but rather active engagement with what it means for daily life. For example, what does it mean to help and defend my neighbor in every necessity of life? What does it mean to interpret charitably all that he does and says? The questions and responses are meant as an introduction to deeper reflection on God's intentions for human life. Remember, too, Luther's encouragement that "after you have taught the people a short catechism like this one, then take up a longer catechism and impart to them a richer and fuller understanding."[15]

Notice also that in Luther's Small Catechism, the explanations to the Ten Commandments do not simply call on the ruling authorities to do something but rather call on the ordinary person to reflect on them, consider what they mean, and live according to them. In his Large Catechism Luther offered longer, thoughtful elucidations of how to and how not to fulfill each commandment.[16] People are seen as moral agents. Implicit in these catechetical discussions of the Ten Commandments

15. The Small Catechism, BC 349.
16. Luther preached on the Ten Commandments many times. See also his *Treatise on Good Works* (1520), TAL 1:257–367.

is an affirmation of ordinary pursuits. Whether they are merchants, farmers, workers, or something else, they hear questions and challenges related to how they carry out their vocations. Consideration of what God's law means is not left to the theologians, civil servants, and canon lawyers.

Implicit, too, in the discussion of the creed is the assumption that ordinary people can learn and understand the work of God. They can distinguish those works—creation, redemption, and sanctification—and reflect on what God does in each. Consideration of who God is and what God does is not left to the theologians.

Reformation-era Lutheran preachers and teachers functioned in a largely oral society. They knew they were teaching the illiterate, but they did not talk down to them. They did not see illiteracy as a barrier to learning, nor did they think illiterate people unworthy of being taught. Sixteenth-century Lutheran pastors expected the illiterate to learn their catechism and thereby evaluate what they were being taught. Addressing a rhetorical question from a listener, Jacob Andreae (1528–1590) explained,

> Yes you say, "I am a layperson, a rough, ignorant person, I can neither write nor read. Who will tell me who preaches correctly or incorrectly, how should I be able to judge this?" Pay attention . . . when you have learned these six main pieces [of the catechism] well, even if you cannot write or read, no erring preacher shall soon lead you astray.[17]

For the Wittenberg Reformers, "mindless repetition" of catechetical content was not the goal. For the Reformers, merely reciting the words of the commandments, creeds, and so forth was not sufficient. Rather, they wanted people to internalize the words and thereby sought to encourage careful reflection on and understanding of the Christian faith as well as active, faithful participation in the life of the civic community and the church.

The Lutheran enterprise of catechizing—whether done by preaching or teaching—assumed the role of pastor is to empower the laity to know the faith and discern its consequences in their lives. Paradoxically, at the same time that he empowered, he also subverted. That is, he subverted any claim that clergy might have the sole authority over reflection on the faith. Do we see pastors today as empowering people and even subverting their own claims? In what ways are laypeople today

---

17. Jacob Andreae, *Zehen Predig von den sechs Hauptstucken Christlicher Lehr (Catechismus genannt) allen Christlichen Hauβva(o)ttern nutzlich zu(o)lesen* . . . (Tübingen: Ulrich Morharts, 1561), 78r.

actively holding pastors (or any authority, inside or outside the church) accountable?

SCHOOLS AND EDUCATION—FOR EVERYONE

The Wittenberg Reformation emphasized the value of education for carrying out one's vocation. The Reformers did not think education merely equipped one to read the Bible. Luther, writing in "To the Councilmen of All Cities in Germany That They Establish and Maintain Christian Schools" (1524), declared,

> Now the welfare of a city does not consist solely in accumulating vast treasures, building mighty walls and magnificent buildings, and producing a goodly supply of guns and armor. Indeed, where such things are plentiful, and reckless fools get control of them, it is so much the worse and the city suffers even great loss. A city's best and greatest welfare, safety, and strength consist rather in its having many able, learned, wise, honorable, and well-educated citizens. They can then readily gather, protect, and properly use treasure and all manner of property.[18]

Philipp Melanchthon, writing in his instructions for the Saxon Visitation of 1527–28, stated, "The preachers are to exhort the people to send their children to school so that persons are educated for competent service both in church and state." And, "Because it is God's will, then, parents should send their children to school, and prepare them for the Lord God so that he may use them for the service of others."[19] Later in those instructions he gave detailed curriculum instructions. In these, he included Christian instruction but rejected the idea that children should be taught only from Scripture, noting, "There are many reasons why also other books beside Scripture should be given the children from which they may learn to speak."[20] In "A Sermon on Keeping Children in School" (1530) Luther described the God-pleasing vocations of those who study law and medicine and urged parents to let their sons study so they can pursue these vocations.[21] Further, he clearly saw it as the duty of ruling authorities to provide schools:

> I hold that it is the duty of the temporal authority to compel its subjects to keep their children in school, especially the promising ones. . . . For

18. Martin Luther, *To the Councilmen of All Cities in Germany That They Establish and Maintain Christian Schools*, in TAL 5:255.

19. Martin Luther, *Instructions for the Visitors of Parish Pastors in Electoral Saxony* (1528), LW 40:314.

20. LW 40:318.

21. LW 46:239–40, 252–53.

it is truly the duty of government to maintain the offices and estates that have been mentioned, so that there will always be preachers, jurists, pastors, writers, physicians, schoolmasters, and the like, for we cannot do without them. If the government can compel such of its subjects as are fit for military service to carry pike and musket, man the ramparts, and do other kinds of work in time of war, how much more can it and should it compel its subjects to keep their children in school. For here there is a worse war on, a war with the very devil, who is out to secretly sap the strength of the cities and principalities, emptying them of their able persons until he has bored out the pith and left only an empty shell of useless people whom he can manipulate and toy with as he will. That is, indeed, to starve out a city or a land and destroy it without a battle, before anyone is even aware of what is going on. The Turk has quite a different approach. He takes every third child in his whole empire and trains it for what he will. How much more ought our lords, then, to take some boys for schooling, since that would not be to take the child away from his parents, but to train him for the benefit of the whole community.[22]

Luther and his fellow Reformers advocated education for everyone, not just the elites of society. Already in 1520, Luther expressed the desire that every town have a girls' school.[23] Andrew Pettegree has called him a "notable pioneer in the field of female education."[24] Pettegree has also noted how subsequent Lutheran church orders supported the cause of female education. He writes:

> The full measure of this achievement can best be gauged if we contrast Lutheran Germany with a survey taken of the schools of Venice in 1587. Venice had many schools with several thousand pupils, but of these girls made up a meager 0.2 percent. *In Germany, in many rural areas, later surveys show that girls made up close to half the enrolled pupils.*[25]

As Pettegree notes, Luther's "real, passionate commitment to female education . . . deserves to be better known."[26]

The antihierarchical tendencies of this advocacy of education are clear. Luther and his fellow Reformers wanted education to be available to all people, not just to elites. They recognized that education would enable

22. LW 46:256–57.

23. "And would God that every town had a girls' school as well, where the girls would be taught the gospel for an hour every day either in German or in Latin." Martin Luther, *To the Christian Nobility of the German Nation Concerning the Improvement of the Christian Estate* (1520), TAL 1:453–54.

24. Andrew Pettegree, *Brand Luther: How an Unheralded Monk Turned His Small Town into a Center of Publishing, Made Himself the Most Famous Man in Europe—and Started the Protestant Reformation* (New York: Penguin, 2015), 265.

25. Pettegree, *Brand Luther*, 266 (emphasis added).

26. Pettegree, *Brand Luther*, 266.

one to carry out one's vocation and participate intelligently in civic life. Education increased the probability that hierarchies in both the civil and the ecclesiastical realm could be held accountable.

BIBLE IN THE VERNACULAR

You may have heard or read that Luther translated the Bible so people could read it in their own language. You will need to correct the picture painted by this—a picture of a pious layperson eagerly (and silently) scrutinizing the biblical text. It's not wrong, but it is incomplete. In the oral society of the sixteenth century, many if not most people *heard* the Bible rather than read it. Luther and the Reformers knew this. They did not think access to the Bible should be limited only to those who could read.

Luther translated the New Testament—and then the Old Testament and the Apocrypha—to be read aloud.[27] On the one hand, he was simply being practical in this regard. Luther knew that most people in his time were illiterate. If he wanted the text of the Bible to be accessible to them, he had to shape his translation to do that. On the other hand, by doing so he showed a great respect for the illiterate. He assumed that they too could hear and understand the biblical message. That message should not be available only to those who possessed the skill of reading. The Bible was meant for all.

Not only did Luther provide the biblical texts in the vernacular, but he also provided aids to help people understand the text. Luther wrote prefaces to the Old and New Testaments and to individual biblical books. He also included annotations in the margins, explaining words or concepts. Luther sought to help readers and hearers understand the text. Again, he assumed that ordinary people could and should understand the message of Scripture.

As time went on, this concern for access—that all people should in some way be able to hear and have available the biblical message—was manifest also in the form of the editions being printed. While initially large folio formats dominated production, with time the small quarto

---

27. Martin Brecht has commented: "The Bible spoke clearly and directly to Luther in the situations of his own life, and he did what he could to transmit that to others. He conceived of the gospel more as an oral message than as a literary text, and this was why his translation took on a spoken character that is picked up by the ear. This led him to select forceful words, succinct expressions, and simple declarative sentences." Martin Brecht, *Martin Luther: Shaping and Defining the Reformation, 1521–1532*, trans. James L. Schaaf (Minneapolis: Fortress Press, 1990), 49.

and octave formats came to dominate.[28] Often, small pamphlet-like editions of individual biblical books were printed. Someone who could not afford to buy an entire Bible could possibly afford one of these.

The Wittenberg Reformers also did not hesitate to use pictures to help them teach the message of the Bible. Whether these pictures were in the Bible, in catechisms, in other works, in stained glass windows, or elsewhere, they were useful aids in teaching. Here again, you see a willingness to teach and empower those who perhaps could not read but who learned in other ways. Luther and his followers wanted all people to hear and understand the message of the Bible. They were ready to use a variety of strategies to aid in reaching this goal.

WORSHIP IN THE VERNACULAR

Consider how the reforms of the worship service empowered laypeople. These reforms meant that ordinary people were no longer viewed as passive recipients of rituals performed by the clergy. Rather, they were seen as active participants in worship, hearing the Word, and responding in prayer, praise, and thanksgiving.

No longer was the celebration of the Eucharist the sole focus of worship, an event that put the spotlight on the priest and the power granted him in ordination. Luther's Reformation emphasized the preached sermon—and, by extension, the ears of people who hear. In fact, Luther wrote that "a Christian congregation should never gather together without the preaching of God's Word and prayer, no matter how briefly. . . . Therefore, when God's Word is not preached, one had better neither sing nor read, or even come together."[29] Luther and the Reformers saw the sermon as a means of grace. God the Holy Spirit is active in the spoken word to create repentance and new life. Luther and the Reformers assumed that all could hear, learn, and understand this message.

Luther and his fellow Reformers also wanted all persons to respond to the proclaimed message in confession and prayer. Writing in *On the Councils and the Church* (1539), Luther included among his seven signs of the church the "prayer, public praise, and thanksgiving to God." He wrote,

> Where you see and hear the Lord's Prayer prayed and taught; or psalms or other spiritual songs sung, in accordance with the word of God and the true

---

28. Mark U. Edwards Jr., *Printing, Propaganda, and Martin Luther* (Minneapolis: Fortress Press, 1994), 126.

29. Martin Luther, *Concerning the Order of Public Worship* (1523), LW 53:11.

faith; also the Creed, the Ten Commandments, and the catechism used in public, you may rest assured that a holy Christian people of God are present. . . . However, we are now speaking of prayers and songs that are intelligible and from which we can learn and by means of which we can mend our ways. The clamor of monks and nuns and priests is not prayer, nor is it praise to God; for they do not understand it, nor do they learn anything from it; they do it like a donkey, only for the sake of the belly and not at all in quest of any reform or sanctification or of the will of God.[30]

The Wittenberg Reformers also knew that ordinary people could themselves proclaim God's Word by singing hymns. Luther wrote in 1523, "I also wish that we had as many songs as possible in the vernacular which the people could sing during mass."[31] As Dorothea Wendebourg has observed, the hymns written by Luther and his followers

> were widely sung inside and outside of churches, in services, in families, in open places, and at work. Thus, they came to be one of the most effective means of propagating the message of the Reformation and, practically from the beginning, one of the distinguishing marks of those congregations that followed the Wittenberg Reformation.[32]

OTHER WAYS OF EMPOWERING

The Wittenberg Reformation empowered people in other respects. One example would be marriage. The Wittenberg Reformation dropped most of the late-medieval church's restrictions on marriage.[33] Though far from adopting the romantic concept of marriage developed in later centuries, Luther firmly believed that no one should be forced to marry someone he or she didn't want to marry. The Wittenberg Reformation also empowered congregations, advocating for their right to select and call their own pastors.[34]

In sum, for the Wittenberg Reformation, no longer were ordinary people viewed as mere recipients of wisdom from on high. They were active, responsible agents. They were to be educated both in the faith and in their vocations to carry out their responsibilities. The Wittenberg

---

30. Martin Luther, *On the Councils and the Church* (1539), TAL 3:430.

31. Martin Luther, *An Order of Mass and Communion for the Church at Wittenberg* (1523), LW 53:36.

32. TAL 4:107.

33. See, e.g., the section on marriage in Luther's *The Babylonian Captivity of the Church* (1520), TAL 3:96–110.

34. Martin Luther, *That a Christian Assembly or Congregation Has the Right and Power to Judge All Teaching and to Call, Appoint, and Dismiss Teachers, Established and Proven by Scripture* (1523), LW 39:301–14.

Reformation believed they should be upheld, encouraged, and aided in those responsibilities.

IMPLICATIONS FOR TODAY

Ordinary people, the "forgotten people" of the sixteenth century, had been looked on as

- engaged in unimportant enterprises—work and family;

- sources of revenue for those further up the societal chain;

- stupid and backward, not worthy of a hearing, and not worth trusting with reflection on the faith;

- needing to have their values changed to conform to and affirm elite values; and

- not worthy of being drawn into the conversation, having their views heard and appreciated.

Luther's Reformation looked at these ordinary, "forgotten people" differently. It saw them as

- people who could know the faith and reflect on it;

- exercising important vocations, vocations in which they could use their gifts and reflect on how best to serve their neighbors; and

- able to learn (about both the faith and those matters needful for their vocations), able to question and think, able themselves to speak and express important thoughts.

The Lutheran Reformation had significant and long-lasting consequences for ordinary people who had been marginalized and, in many respects, forgotten in church and society. Those who claim the heritage of the Lutheran Reformation need to remember and reflect on this. An engagement with our past leads us to ask important questions today. Who are the forgotten people in our society? Whom have the elites forgotten? Can those of us teaching and studying this book exhibit the same care and respect for the forgotten people that Luther and his fellow Reformers did? Do we want to empower them? Listen respectfully to their insights? Take the risk of encouraging them through education to engage more deeply in their vocations? Engage them in serious discussions about the future of our society? Or do we simply want to dictate to them? Feel self-righteously superior? Empowerment is risky. Those whom we empower may have very different perspectives than we do. They may also offer new suggestions and solutions to pressing problems in our churches and society. Are we willing to do the hard work and take the risk of empowering people?

4.

Reclaiming an Ethic of Care in Luther's Theology of Embodiment

WANDA DEIFELT

Martin Luther's ethics can be summarized by his reflection on Christian life: Christians live not in themselves but in Christ and in their neighbor. Living in Christ through faith and in their neighbor through love, they give witness to the word of God. By faith, Christians are, as Luther says, "caught up beyond themselves" into God. By love, they reach out beyond themselves toward their neighbor.[1] In faith and love, they act out Jesus's great commandment, bringing God and neighbor together into the ethical living of believers: "Love the Lord your God with all your heart, and with all your soul, and with all your mind, and with all your strength," and "love your neighbor as yourself" (Mark 12:30–31). Just as God extends care toward humanity, human beings ought to extend care to each other. However, too often this care for the neighbor focuses on the afterlife, emphasizing the soul over the body and reducing Christianity to the spiritual realm.

CHRISTIAN ETHICS AND BODIES

Recalling the doctrine of justification by faith, many believers tend to downplay the importance of good works in Luther's theology. A common misinterpretation is that if we are justified by faith through grace, there is no need for any effort on our part. Being justified exempts us from the need to perform good works. This assumption is both wrong and highly problematic, because it makes Christians lose sight of their

---

1. Martin Luther, *The Freedom of a Christian*, in *Martin Luther: Selections from His Writings*, ed. John Dillenberger (New York: Anchor, 1962), 80.

faith's prophetic impetus and fail to announce the good news of God's grace to a suffering world. It often reduces Christianity to a private, spiritual, and eschatological concern focused only on salvation and the afterlife. The community-wide approach is lost, and the importance of Jesus's discipleship for the here and now is denied. At the root of the problem is a dualism between body and soul, where concerns of the soul are ranked higher than material needs and everyday struggles. This has tremendous effects on the care of bodies—whether it be human bodies, the social body of communities, or the body of creation.[2] The focus of Christian ministry on the salvation of souls and the afterlife diminishes the need for advocacy, compassion, and justice-seeking efforts in the here and now.

This body-soul dualism affects the way human bodies are perceived in contemporary society as well.[3] On the one hand, we deny the experience of human bodies—especially suffering, famished, ill, and violated bodies. We become insensitive, or even anesthetized, to other people's pain, because suffering is often presented as a caricature and as if it were an ephemeral manner. Everyday violence (either conveyed through mass media or experienced though encounters with others) has even become a source of entertainment. However, repeated exposure to violence gradually sweeps away empathy and care. When the care of bodies is not a Christian concern, dismissal of other people's needs and the needs of the planet becomes acceptable. In this context, it is not surprising that the spiritual dimension—and the salvation of the soul (one's own)—becomes the primary focus of Christian teaching. This focus obfuscates the care for creation and the ethical concern for the well-being of the neighbor, who has bodily needs for food, drink, shelter, clothing, and overall quality of life.

On the other hand, we are often obsessed with bodies, especially our own human body, at the expense of the well-being of the social body and the body of creation. This behavior leads to unequal distribution of resources, climate change, pollution, the destruction of natural habitats, and the extinction of other species. The objectification of human bodies through mass media, the commercial use of bodies (particularly women's bodies) to advertise products, the exploitation of bodies through sex tourism, and the overall preoccupation with making human bodies fit an

2. This chapter focuses primarily on the lack of care for human bodies, but a more comprehensive approach to the social body and the body of creation can be found in Wanda Deifelt, "And G*d Saw That It Was Good: *Imago Dei* and Its Challenge to Climate Justice," in *Planetary Solidarity: Global Women's Voices on Christian Doctrine and Climate Justice*, ed. Grace Ji-Sun Kim and Hilda P. Koster (Minneapolis: Fortress Press, 2017), 119–32.

3. Marga J. Stroeher, Wanda Deifelt, and Andre S. Musskopf, *À Flor da Pele: Ensaios Sobre Gênero e Corporeidade* (São Leopoldo: Sinodal, 2004).

established aesthetic mold are contemporary symptoms of the denial of real bodies. Bodies that do not conform to norms about gender, physical mobility, weight, color, or age are stigmatized. The need to conform to a stereotypical body model (or mold) leads people to subject themselves to surgeries and diets that jeopardize rather than ensure physical well-being. They punish their bodies in order to comply with the values a culture imposes. Overindulgence in bodily pleasures (overeating or overdrinking, for instance), guided by instant pleasure, is an additional product of this hedonistic approach.

While it is correct that good works have no place when it comes to salvation, good works are an important part of Christian life. Our love of neighbor can be expressed only through good works, extending concrete care toward physical beings. This holistic quest for the well-being of bodies—in their personal, social, and environmental dimensions—is embodied care. Embodiment refers to the interactions of various bodies and the multiple realms in which they occur, such as the human body with itself (what we learn from our own bodies), the influence of the social body on individual bodies (through social and cultural constraints), or the effect of social bodies on the body of creation (the results of human action in terms of deforestation, pollution, and so forth). These interactions happen on multiple levels. Embodiment keeps us real, relational, vulnerable, and interdependent beings. It is through our bodies that we communicate, interact, and demonstrate our care for each other. Luther states, "Our body is a sort of house, in which both the political and the domestic may be found."[4] If our body is a house the spirit inhabits, then our bodies are communal sites of love and grace.

Embodiment not only provides the vehicle for us to practice Christian love. It is where this love is manifested. Embodied care reclaims the importance of bodies in our theological reflection and ethical deliberation. The Gospels convey this message and spell out its real implications: the divine enters human reality and becomes fully embodied. The consequence of this truth is witnessed in the ministry of Jesus: his miracles, healing, feeding, preaching, and reintegrating the outcast back into the community. In his daily life, Jesus taught what he meant by the abundant life and invited his followers to carry out the same ministry he did, standing with the poor and oppressed. It is astonishing that the embodied care promulgated by Jesus could be viewed as a private and spiritual message, as if Jesus's ministry related to the salvation of only souls and not of bodies.

4. Martin Luther, "Notes on Ecclesiastes," LW 15:179.

DISMISSAL OF HUMAN BODIES

Christianity has always had a complicated relationship with bodies. On the one hand, the Hebrew/Semitic tradition understands the human body as part of God's good creation. Because humans are made in the image of God, bodies need to be treated with respect and dignity. In some instances, this might require laws that ensure purity and keep impurity afar (thus regulating our treatment of bodies). On the other hand, in Greco-Roman approaches, the body is either kept under control through ascetic practices or overly indulged with orgies and bacchanals.[5] In the Greco-Roman setting, the body is considered inferior to the immaterial world. It requires submission and control. Best-known is Plato's view of the body as the prison of the soul. The body, a carcass, prevents the immortal soul from being free. Death is welcomed because it allows the soul to be liberated. The body could perish, but the soul would live.[6]

In the New Testament, Paul's theology is the epitome of the tension between positive and negative views of embodiment. Paul even uses two different words to denote human physicality. When the body is good, it is called *sōma*; when it is bad, it is called *sarx*. But in his attempt to regulate the body, Paul also reveals his own biases. For instance, in 1 Corinthians 6:15–20, he seems to treat the body with the greatest dignity, describing it as the temple of the Holy Spirit (v. 19). But the body does not always maintain this status, as it can be corrupted. Paul writes,

> Do you not know that your bodies are members of Christ? Should I therefore take the members of Christ and make them members of a prostitute? Never! Do you not know that whoever is united to a prostitute becomes one body with her? For it is said, "The two shall be one flesh." But anyone united to the Lord becomes one spirit with him. Shun fornication! Every sin that a person commits is outside the body; but the fornicator sins against the body itself. Or do you not know that your body is a temple of the Holy Spirit within you, which you have from God, and that you are not your own? For you were bought with a price; therefore glorify God in your body. (1 Cor 6:16–20)

The message Paul conveys is that, while the human body is sacred because it is the temple of the Holy Spirit, not all bodies are equal. Paul identifies certain actions that, in his view, corrupt the body, such as

---

5. Frank Bottomley, *Attitudes to the Body in Western Christianity* (London: Lepus, 1979), 3–15.
6. Brian K. Harvey, *Daily Life in Ancient Rome: A Sourcebook* (Indianapolis: Hackett, 2016), 314–23.

prostitution and fornication. Ironically, Paul creates a hierarchy among bodies: those that are pure and those, such as the prostitute's, that are impure. He juxtaposes the "members of Christ" and the "members of a prostitute" to show that contact with tarnished or sullied bodies is sinful. In doing so, the inherent goodness of the body, as a temple of the Holy Spirit, seems to get lost in light of the poor choices regarding one's sexual life or moral standards (by engaging in fornication, adultery, extramarital sex, and so forth). This distinction is problematic because it labels some bodies as less worthy of dignity and respect, since the body of the prostitute is no longer the temple of the Holy Spirit. Through his pejorative remarks about the body of the prostitute, Paul furthers the bias of the Greco-Roman culture, namely, the bodies of slaves, women, children, and those deemed barbarian are of lesser value than the bodies of the free, propertied, male citizen.

This hierarchy of bodies supplants Jesus's own ministry, in which he treats with respect and dignity bodies assailed by blindness, leprosy, hunger, or demons. Jesus addresses the adulterous woman with mercy and shows favor to prostitutes and tax collectors. Paul, rather, reinstates the dualities and hierarchies that already existed in the Greco-Roman world, deeming some bodies more important than others. This view served as a framework for future generations, imposing on them the values of empire, colonialism, slavery, heterosexism, and gender stereotyping. As consequence, in the following centuries, Christianity was used to perpetuate inequalities: The body of the prostitute is less worthy than the body of the virgin. The body of the black person is less valuable than the body of a white person. The body of a homeless, drug-addicted, poor woman is less important than that of a college student.

This hierarchy of bodies goes against the grain of Jesus's message of care to ensure physical and spiritual well-being. It dismisses the baptismal theology annotated by Paul himself in Galatians 3:27–28: "As many of you as were baptized into Christ have clothed yourselves with Christ. There is no longer Jew or Greek, there is no longer slave or free, there is no longer male and female; for all of you are one in Christ Jesus." The baptismal formula of the early church defended that even if society created hierarchies based on characteristics of one's body—whether it be one's sexuality, social status, skin color, or ethnicity—this would not be the case in the church. Nevertheless, once Christianity got co-opted by the Roman Empire and became the official religion of the colonial enterprise, the equality advocated through baptism was postponed as an eschatological reality.

This does not mean, however, that Christianity has nothing to say about bodies. To the contrary. Already in the early church, many church fathers such as Jerome, Tertullian, and Augustine described the body as the main locus for evil, a source of temptation, and a reason to sin.[7] Women's bodies, in particular, were targeted by patriarchal rhetoric, blaming Eve for the presence of sin in the world and alleging that she was the second in the order of creation but the first one to disobey God's command. At the core of these views is not advocacy for the well-being of bodies but objectification of bodies, the use of bodies to justify further oppression and discrimination.

Similarly, contemporary debates on embodiment are quite disembodied: sexuality is reduced to debates over homosexuality instead of sexuality as a constitutive part of the human experience. Discussions about sexual education, contraception, and safe sex are limited to debate (or lack thereof) on abortion and abstinence. Ensuring access to preventive medicine and health care is described as a political agenda. Guaranteeing the survival of migrants, refugees, and asylum seekers is labeled a threat to national security. The well-being of bodies is not seen in a holistic manner. Rather, the concern for the body is reduced to a single matter, and this one aspect (whether it be homosexuality, abortion, immigration, or other issues) is disproportionately addressed though preestablished moralistic and individualistic principles.

African American, liberation, feminist, womanist, mujerista, and queer theologians have strongly criticized this travesty of Christianity, because it has served as a justification for enslaving, raping, and lynching those whose bodies are deemed less valuable and less dignified. We live in a world in which women's bodies can be sexually assaulted and objectified. We are enmeshed in a rape culture that shames victims and survivors of abuse instead of those who violate bodies. Today, we live in a world in which black and brown bodies are imprisoned at a much higher rate than white bodies. Ours is a world where frail, aging, broken, ill, and homeless bodies are punished for their vulnerability, and access to health care is a privilege granted only to those who can afford it.

When human bodies are not honored, violence is tolerated. The lack of regard for human bodies leads to abuse and perpetuates injustice, as denounced by two current social movements, MeToo (#MeToo) and Black Lives Matter (#BlackLivesMatter). The widespread prevalence of harassment and sexual assault in the workplace, as revealed by the MeToo movement, and the violence inflicted on African American communities by the state and vigilantes, as demonstrated by Black Lives Matter, raise awareness about the collective effect that the lack of care for bodies engenders. These movements remind us of the need to denounce

7. See, e.g., Hannah Hunt, *Clothed in the Body: Asceticism, the Body and the Spiritual in the Late Antique Era* (Burlington, VT: Ashgate, 2012).

the atrocities committed and become catalysts for social transformation. If the mistreatment of bodies is indicative of abuse and injustice, then the prophetic and transformative power of faith requires us to address, denounce, and change it. When human bodies are respected and honored, justice abounds.

BODIES IN MARTIN LUTHER'S THEOLOGY

Although Luther sometimes refers to the body as a "rotten old bag" and admonishes that it be kept under control, he does not promote a hierarchy (that a Christian should pay attention to the soul and not to the body, for instance). For Luther, the dualism between soul and body is pointless because to tend to the needs of the body is to also pay attention to the soul. Luther writes, "Body and soul present two distinct entities in a natural and sound person; yet the two constitute but one person, and we ascribe the functions, activities, and offices of each to the whole person."[8] He perceives the spirit as the deepest part of the human being, the body its exterior manifestation, and the soul as the source of life. It is in the interaction of bodies and how we treat our own body that we live out the goodness of God's creation.

However, Luther often repeats the concept of embodiment articulated by Paul, where he distinguishes between the body as intrinsically good and the flesh as corrupt. For Luther, embodiment is not bad. Rather, it reflects the tension between humanity as God's embodied creation and the brokenness of our ways. Christians are always faced with both the experience of justice and peace and the reality of sin and temptation that leads away from that path.[9] Luther writes,

> Just as we should not be cruel to other people's bodies or trouble them with unjust requirements, so we should not do this to our own bodies either. According to Paul's command, therefore, we should make provisions for our flesh, to enable it . . . to meet its needs, not "to gratify its desires."[10]

For Luther, all resources stem from God, from whom life itself springs. In our bodies and through them, we experience God. The world God created is at the same time the occasion and the place for gratitude. The

8. Martin Luther, *Sermons on the Gospel of St. John Chapters 14–16*, LW 24:106.

9. This paradox is exemplified in the following quote: "A living sacrifice is a body which is afflicted for the Lord, and it is called living sacrifice because it lives in virtues and is dead to vices; it is a sacrifice because it is already dead to this world and its depraved works; living because all the things it continues are good." Martin Luther, *Lectures on Romans: Glosses and Scholia*, LW 25:436.

10. Martin Luther, *Lectures on Galatians*, LW 27:69.

whole creation is an opportunity to encounter God. All that we touch, see, hear, smell, taste, sense, and feel must

> be traced back to God, because they are gifts of God put into practice not only in the spirit but also outside and toward people; for God is also the God of bodies. Therefore he provides us with bodily gifts, and he wants us to enjoy these gifts with gladness.[11]

The goodness of God's creation is manifested in and through our bodies, for God is a God of bodies. For this reason, God provides everything we need to tend for our bodies and care for our neighbors' bodies: food, shelter, good weather, government, spouse and parents, health, and peace.

> How angry can God really be if He lets His sun rise for us every day, if He gives us good weather, if He lets all kinds of plants, fruits, and nourishment grow for us, if He favors us with healthy bodies and members? If we could look at these things properly, we would have to say: "He surely has given us great treasures—above all, peace and joy toward Him and, in addition, all kinds of physical benefactions on earth, visible and palpable evidence of His mercy and His willingness to help us."[12]

Such divine gifts are not an entitlement; that is, that we cannot take them for granted, as possessions. God has no obligation to provide us with them. A sense of entitlement is disrespectful, the attitude of those who do not see life and creation as gifts. To squander natural resources, to lose one's sense of awe, to objectify the material world, or to turn it into a commodity is sinful. Entitlement claims excessive power for humanity rather than God, the Creator. Our dependence on God's grace is not only a matter of faith but applies also to material matters. We pray that God will sustain and maintain us. In doing so, we recognize that we depend on God. We also give thanks to God for bestowing good things onto us. This prayerful and thankful attitude is similar to Luther's interpretation of the fourth petition in the Lord's Prayer: "Give us today our daily bread." The good we have is due to God and is to be used for the purpose of praising God. Once material things become the center of our concerns, mammon, and not God, rules.

> But the same truth declares also and teaches that you should let such good things go, be ready at all times to do without them, if God so wills it, and cleave to God alone. The truth, by saying they are good, does not compel you to take the good things back again, nor to say that they are not good;

---

11. Martin Luther, *Lectures on Genesis*, LW 4:273.
12. Luther, *Sermons on the Gospel of St. John Chapters 14–16*, LW 24:180.

but it does compel you to regard them with equanimity and to confess that they are good and not evil.[13]

When Luther states that God is also a God of bodies, he redefines medieval theology and spirituality. In the Middle Ages, life was brutish and short, and celibacy was considered a good work, meriting divine reward. Monastic life required denial of the human body and its sexual desires in favor of what the Roman Church deemed to be higher aspirations: the salvation of souls. Luther does not spare criticism of these ideas. In reclaiming the body as God's good creation, Luther asserts that human sexuality should not be denied, but embraced. It should be lived out in a healthy, respectful, mutually engaging, and caring manner. Christians ought not shy away from addressing issues of sexuality but see it as a gift.

Even if Luther critiques bodily misconduct, he also affirms that those who live chaste lives are in no way more pure than anybody else: "In this world we are bound by the needs of our bodily life, but we are not righteous because of them."[14] Again, Luther's notion of *simul iustus et peccator* is relevant; everybody is always saint and sinner. Nobody is better or worse than anybody else. Luther's theology criticizes the ascetic, monastic misunderstanding that one worships God only through denial of the material world: "Is it not true that money, property, body, spouse, child, friends, and the like are good things created and given by God Himself?"[15] They are God's gifts to us. It is in this material realm that Christians both experience temptation and are called into concrete works of love. This is the arena of God's action, where believers testify their faith not by judging each other but by caring for one another.

LUTHERAN ETHICS AS EMBODIED CARE

Living out our faith is a daily exercise, and Martin Luther uses his sermons and writings to educate church members about the ethical consequences of Christian life. In 1521, he wrote a commentary on the Magnificat (Luke 1:46–55) in which he extols God's grace toward Mary and her own legacy of instruction and example for Christians. He dedicated his commentary to John Frederick, the seventeen-year-old son of the Elector John of Saxony. Luther believed that the message of the Magnificat should be a guideline for all princes, lords, and all who are in leadership position because it compels them to be humble and seek

---

13. Martin Luther, *The Magnificat*, LW 21:335.
14. Luther, *The Freedom of a Christian*, LW 31:373.
15. Luther, *The Magnificat*, LW 21:334.

the common good. They should not boast or be prideful, defending their own interests. Rather, their vocation as God's servants is to protect those in need. Because leaders often think they answer to nobody, the Magnificat reminds them that, in fact, they have to answer to an even higher power, namely God.

For Luther, the Magnificat is a statement of both personal and political ethics. Because material resources are God's gifts to us, individuals as well as government have the responsibility of ensuring that these gifts (resources) be shared. Temporal power is duty bound to defend its subject, seeking not its own but its neighbor's profit and God's honor.[16] Luther articulates this in his teachings regarding the two kingdoms. God rules the world in two ways. God rules the worldly (or left-hand) kingdom through secular authority, by means of law. God rules the heavenly (or right-hand) kingdom through the gospel, by means of grace. Thus, to ensure that justice prevails on earth, God instituted good governance. That is why we ask for God's presence in every dimension of our existence, from daily bread to a just government.[17]

The role of the government is to see that the needs of all citizens are met: "The government has the charge not to permit the harsh oppression of the innocent."[18] Christians are called to service, to make sure the government acts justly. A Christian has not only the opportunity but also the obligation to advocate on the behalf of others (the neighbor). Luther's two kingdom doctrine has consequences for the way Christians perceive themselves and act in society—the social body to which we belong. Christians are active citizens, taking responsibility and being accountable for the common good. In doing so, they embody Christ and become Christ to the world.

> Thus Christ and the Christians become one loaf and one body, so that the Christian can bear good fruit—not Adam's or his own, but Christ's. For when a Christian baptizes, preaches, consoles, exhorts, works, and suffers, he does not do this as a man descended from Adam; it is Christ who does this in him. The lips and tongue with which he proclaims and confesses God's Word are not his; they are Christ's lips and tongue. The hands with which

16. Luther, *The Magnificat*, LW 21:337.
17. "We should pray God to grant us the blessing of peace and a good government and to protect us from all kinds of trouble, from sickness and pestilence, from famine and bloodshed and bad weather. You are not beyond the reach of death yet, nor have you eaten up all your daily bread; hence you dare not stop praying for Him to give it to you daily. Similarly, because daily . . . you have to go on praying in support of the government and in opposition to vices of every sort and the tendency of people to rob and steal from one another." Martin Luther, *The Sermon on the Mount*, LW 21:231.
18. Luther, *Sermon on the Mount*, LW 21:25.

he toils and serves his neighbor are the hands and members of Christ, who, as He says here, is in him; and he is in Christ.[19]

Jesus commands the love of neighbor. Human beings, however, need to be constantly reminded of this imperative. If we depended on ourselves, we would look out only for what is good for us, our family, or friends. The egotistical and self-centered character of humanity prevents us from fully accomplishing the love of neighbor on our own. Either because we would falsely believe such good works would be used for our own merit or because we would reduce the neighbor's needs to our own interests, true good works can spring only from justification itself. The use of the law in the theological or spiritual sense—when it refers to one's salvation—is condemned. Still, the law has a positive and necessary theological use because it reminds humans that we are self-centered creatures, full of pride and eager to justify ourselves through our own good deeds.

Even if Christians are justified by faith through grace, the fulfillment of the law in its civic or political use is a requirement for all Christians because it guides, compels, protects, and leads to good works.[20] In this sense, Lutheran ethics is political not because it is partisan but because it is concerned with the common good. The law, therefore, is not only good and necessary, but it is also given by God. It is the basis for a just society and serves as a constant reminder of our social responsibilities. It locates us in our social relationships in family, work, church, country, and as global citizens.[21] Christians, therefore, are justice-seeking beings, working for the well-being of others.

19. Luther, *Sermons on the Gospel of St. John Chapters 14–16*, LW 24:226.

20. Martin Luther, *Commentary on St. Paul's Epistle to the Galatians*, in Dillenberger, *Martin Luther*, 139–45.

21. Luther summarizes his position in the following way: "Christians, among themselves and by and for themselves, need no law or sword, since it is neither necessary nor profitable for them. Since, however, a true Christian lives and labors on earth not for himself but for his neighbor, therefore the whole spirit of his life impels him to do even that which he need not do, but which is profitable and necessary for his neighbor. Because the sword is a very great benefit and necessary to the whole world, to preserve peace, to punish sin and to prevent evil, he submits most willingly to the rule of the sword, pays tax, honors those in authority, serves, helps, and does all he can to further the government, that it may be sustained and held in honor and fear. Although he needs none of these things for himself and it is not necessary for him to do them, yet he considers what is for the good and profit of others, as Paul teaches in Ephesians 5:21." Martin Luther, *Secular Authority: To What Extent It Should Be Obeyed*, in Dillenberger, *Martin Luther*, 373.

According to Luther, faith springs into acts of love. Christians seek the well-being of their neighbor not only because to do so is the law (a divine commandment) but also in freedom, out of love. Good works are concrete expressions of Christian service. A Christian becomes free to serve. Christian vocation includes taking an active role in political affairs and works of advocacy out of genuine concern for the well-being of others. Ethical reflection, from a Lutheran perspective, encompasses our effort to acknowledge the rights of others as God's creatures, placing us as instruments of God's love and requiring us to carry out good works on behalf of others. It stems from a grateful attitude, due to the notion that we live through the grace of God. By serving the other, one's neighbor, one is also serving Christ. As Luther explains in his "Preface to the New Testament":

> [The believer] confesses and teaches this gospel to the people at the risk of life itself. His whole life and all his effort are directed towards the benefit of his neighbor, and this not just in order to help him to attain the same grace; but he employs his strength, uses his goods, and stakes his reputation, as he sees Christ did for him and therefore follows His example. Christ never gave any other commandment than that of love, because He intended that commandment to be the test of His disciples and of true believers. For if [good] works and love do not blossom forth, it is not genuine faith, the gospel has not yet gained a foothold, and Christ is not yet rightly known.[22]

Although the core of Luther's theology on good works is quite clear—and its importance undeniable—it is still surprising how easily this perspective becomes abstract or its scope reduced to charitable actions. The concern for the well-being of neighbor, as Luther spells out, is the basis for an ethics of care. To care for another human being is to ensure dignity and life in abundance, act for justice and peace, and enable another to flourish as a full human being created in the image of God. It implies a genuine concern for the neighbor's needs. The neighbor is the other with whom I engage as an equal, the one who brings me closer to Christ, and the one I am Christ for.

This ethics of care is embodied because it compels us to pay close attention to the personal and social bodies as well as the body of creation. The body is such a strong image that Paul uses it as a metaphor to describe the church—the body of Christ. This is a reminder that bodies can also be relational, collective, and communal. The ethical implications for this ecclesiology are remarkable: "If one member suffers, all suffer together with it; if one member is honored, all rejoice together with

---

22. Martin Luther, *Preface to the New Testament*, in Dillenberger, *Martin Luther*, 18.

it" (1 Cor 12:26).[23] The church, as the body of Christ, is more than an assembly of bodies. It is Christ's real presence in each person, affirming mutually in each person's dignity and creative potentiality. It is also affirmed through baptism, whereby Christians become one in Christ (Gal 3:27–28). To become part of the body, through baptism, means that each body is respected in its individuality. The body of Christ, the church, respects the different talents given to each member by the Holy Spirit, recognizing diversity itself as a gift.[24] To care for the members of the body is to voice the suffering and the joys of each body and the collective body as well.

The core of Christian ethics is care for the well-being of neighbor. This well-being includes bodily safety, nourishment, and shelter. This ethic includes employing our strength, goods, and reputation to advocate on behalf of others. Such advocacy is not based on the merits of the neighbor or our own merit, but is carried out through service, in love and care. This neighbor may or may not be part of the body of Christ, the church. After all, Christian hospitality is not extended only to other Christians. Christian vocation is a call to be responsible for the well-being of others, the stranger, the alien, the neighbor: "It is one's neighbor, not one's sanctification, which stands at the heart of the ethics of vocation."[25] To respond to the needs of others is more than intervention in situations of peril. A Christian is an enabler, an advocate, a spokesperson for the rights of others, a doer of good deeds, an agent of transformation, a bearer of peace, and a proclaimer of justice.

As Luther states, "The body is a beautiful and noble creation of God."[26] Therefore, it is also our responsibility to ensure the well-being of bodies. We cannot save souls, since salvation is a prerogative of God alone. But we can, and must, work for the well-being of each other's bodies and everything that this entails: food, shelter, clothing, education, and the like. This is the realm of Christian action: to do good works on behalf of others, to ensure the good of one's neighbor and not merely one's

23. Luther affirms interdependence, recognizing that the community lives through its members and compensates for each other's flaws and shortcomings: "Again there are those who see that they are honorable and serve as a cover for others and as a result run away from the others to whom they have been given a cloak of respectability. These are the most foolish of all, because they think that they are this way of themselves, not realizing that they are what they are because of other people." Luther, *Lectures on Romans*, LW 25:510.

24. "*For as one body*, the body is a unit, as is also the church, *we are many members*, yet the many members do not divide the unity, thus neither do the many believers divide the church, *and all*, that is, the individual, *the members do not have the same function*, the same duty, as in 1 Cor. 12:4ff." Luther, *Lectures on Romans*, LW 25:105–6.

25. Gustaf Wingren, *Luther on Vocation*, trans. Carl C. Rasmussen (1957; repr., Eugene, OR: Wipf & Stock, 2004), 182.

26. Luther, *Sermons on the Gospel of St. John Chapters 14–16*, LW 24:206.

own. To serve one's neighbor—to genuinely care for her or him and ensure his or her well-being—is to reclaim embodiment. We practice this care in concrete ways. We care for the physical and spiritual well-being of others and foster relationships that reflect the belief that we are God's creation, redeemed and reconciled in Christ, and called forth to announce good news and practice good works.

5.

Reclaiming the Legacies of Martin Luther and James Baldwin in Fighting Racism

ANTHONY BATEZA

The work of remembering Martin Luther can easily become parochial, providing Lutherans today with another opportunity to talk to one another about their forebear and namesake. While such exercises are not without merit, the danger is that we will simply be muttering to ourselves in the corner instead of actively engaging others in dialogue. This danger is particularly troubling when we consider the pressing social issues we face. In this essay, then, I will be placing Martin Luther into conversation with the author and social critic James Baldwin, asking how a rich theological tradition might provide us with tools to name and confront racism in the world today.

I approach this topic with the full knowledge that I am writing as a person of color within the Evangelical Lutheran Church in America (ELCA), a denomination that ended the previous century as a church body that was overwhelmingly white and that continues to be so in the opening decades of this century. I acknowledge this reality because it provides the context for, and gives shape to, what follows. While the ELCA includes people from a myriad of backgrounds, I am writing primarily to white folks surrounded by other white folks in pews across this nation. As such I will not directly be addressing the important and Spirit-filled work of people of color in congregations large and small across the church.

This essay begins by briefly discussing how racism operates at the individual and structural levels, arguing that Luther's own analysis of sin and responsibility can help us capture how racism is both a personal and public evil. From here, I will mine Luther's theology of baptism and confession for insights into identity and honesty. Once I have sufficiently engaged Luther, I will look to Baldwin as one who helps us see how these insights can be embodied in public witness. Finally, because the challenges we face and the solutions we need lie not only in the past, I will conclude with a brief set of practical recommendations for ways Christians who embrace Luther's heritage might make use of his insights in congregations.

WHAT *IS* RACISM?

Conversations about racism are not an uncommon feature of contemporary life in the United States. We find ourselves in heated debates with relatives at Thanksgiving about the former National Football League quarterback Colin Kapernick's decision to respectfully kneel during the national anthem in protest of police brutality or bracing for the latest news about racial profiling in coffee shops or police shootings on back patios. Even in today's political climate, most non-Tiki-torch-wielding Americans grant that racism is wrong, an evil to be identified and denounced.[1] What is often lacking in these conversations, however, is serious time defining and discussing what racism *is*. Because of this lack of clarity, I fear that we are often talking past each other. As we address this concern, I recommend we approach an understanding of racism from at least two vantage points, one individual and the other sociostructural.[2]

The individual or personal account of racism tends to focus on a persons' bad beliefs, emotions, and actions. The concern here is primarily the motives and habits that cause people to view and treat others in unjust ways, to not give another what he or she is due. The injustice

---

1. The allusion here is, of course, to the "Unite the Right" rally that took place in Charlottesville, Virginia, the weekend of August 11–12, 2017. While the gathering was ostensibly about the removal of a statue honoring the Confederate general Robert E. Lee, violence quickly erupted between various groups of white supremacists and the counterprotesters who gathered to denounce racism and the monument. The death of Heather Heyer, who was struck down by a Neo-Nazi who drove his car into a crowd, and the images of young white men wielding Tiki torches and hurling racial slurs, came to define the event.

2. I am greatly reducing and simplifying a complicated conversation about how to define and understand racism. Some approaches, like the one embraced by Kwame Anthony Appiah, view racism as fundamentally intellectual, we might say errors in judgment. Racists have mistaken beliefs about people in various racial or ethnic groups, and they resist abandoning these beliefs even in the face of contradictory evidence. Jorge Garcia, in contrast, has offered an account of racism that emphasizes the will and our emotional states over our ideas or beliefs, such that racism is only present where a person acts out of hatred or wishes another ill. See Kwame Anthony Appiah, "Racisms," in *Anatomy of Racism*, ed. David Theo Goldberg (Minneapolis: University of Minnesota Press, 1990); and Jorge Garcia, "The Heart of Racism," *Journal of Social Philosophy* 27, no. 1 (1996): 5–45.

could be large or small, a violent hate crime or a "microaggression" in which subtle verbal and nonverbal actions treat people of color as inferior or unwelcome, with the emphasis falling on the explicit and implicit biases about another person's racial or ethnic identity.[3] It may not be important that such bad behavior comes packaged with malicious motivations. One can recognize that some racists act out of simple ignorance or, in more serious cases, believe that racists' actions actually improve the lives of all people. Here we might think of paternalistic and misguided claims that de facto segregation in public schools really benefits both white and black students as each group is able to better relate with others from their own ethnic or racial group.[4]

Approached from another direction, while there are serious issues with the errors in individual belief, feeling, and action, the real challenges of racism are found in larger social institutions and forces.[5] The social explanation goes as follows. Racism entails the production or maintenance of systems of domination based on racial categories. These systems of domination encompass various areas of life—psychological, education, economic, and political.[6]

The relationship between individual and systemic racism is not unidirectional; individuals are shaped by and, in turn, reshape racist structures. As the sociologist Eduardo Bonilla-Silva puts it, "The central component of any dominant racial ideology is its frames or *set pathways for interpreting information*. These set paths operate as cul-de-sacs because after people filter issues through them, they explain racial phenomena following a predictable route."[7] Put simply, racist systems and patterns

3. For more on the science behind the idea of implicit bias, see Anthony Greenwald and Linda Hamilton Krieger, "Implicit Bias: Scientific Foundations," *California Law Review* 94, no. 4 (2006): 945–68.

4. Throughout this chapter I will elide the important differences, and debates, surrounding the terms *race* and *ethnicity*.

5. I draw on the work of Michael Omi and Howard Winat, *Racial Formation in the United States*, 3rd ed. (New York: Routledge, 2015).

6. As Eduardo Bonilla-Silva defines it, the term "racialized social systems . . . refers to societies in which economic, political, social, and ideological levels are partially structured by the placement of actors in racial categories or races. . . . In all racialized social systems the placement of people in racial categories involves some form of hierarchy that produces definite social relations between the races. The race placed in the superior position tends to receive great economic remuneration and access to better occupations and/or prospects in the labor market, occupies a primary position in the political system, is granted higher social estimation (e.g., is viewed as 'smarter' or 'better looking'), often has the license to draw physical (segregation) as well as social (racial etiquette) boundaries between itself and other races, and receives what DuBois calls a 'psychological wage.' The totality of these racialized social relations and practices constitutes the racial structure of a society." See Eduardo Bonilla-Silva, "Rethinking Racism: Toward a Structural Interpretation," *American Sociological Review* 62, no. 3 (June 1997): 469–70.

7. Bonilla-Silva, interested in colorblind racism, identified four frames operative in the United States today: abstract liberalism, naturalization, cultural racism, and the minimization of

of thought organize human relationships and shape identity in ways that
we are often unaware of, in much the same way that the roads we drive
on both guide and constrain our travel.

While we can distinguish viewing racism as a personal, moral failing
from the approach that sees it as a larger institutional or structural
apparatus, we need not play these two approaches against each other.
Structures, after all, do not have some reified existence apart from the
individual agents who live within them. Likewise, we cannot view
individuals as unique islands that are untethered from the larger social
structures that have contributed to their formation. Combined, we can
say that racism is a social ill, a disease of the larger communal body whose
symptoms manifest in the behaviors of individuals and the operations
of systems. Staying with the body metaphor, the individual and the
systemic reinforce one another in a feedback loop, meaning that our
treatment options will require individual and societal interventions.

LUTHER ON SIN

For those of us who look to Luther for guidance, there is an important
resonance between this approach to racism and Luther's views about
sin in the community. While there is a danger in overusing the word
dialectical, it is fair to say that in many areas Luther seeks to bring
and hold together what might otherwise appear to be opposing or
contradictory positions. When it comes to sin, then, we can see Luther
holding together an uncompromising account of our radical corruption
as individual sinners who fail to trust God and the ways in which our
broken relationships and institutions breed corruption.[8] One place in
Luther's thought where this tension comes out is in his discussion of evil
in the malformation of political leaders.

In his 1534 *Commentary on Psalm 101*, written as a mirror for Elector
John Frederick, Luther emphasizes a point that he made repeatedly
throughout his career: in general, rulers are presumptuous people,
overconfident in their abilities and often confusing temporary success
with divine blessing.[9] Even when there are blessed and good rulers
like King David and Emperor Maximilian I (1459–1519), it is often
the case that such individuals have great difficulty finding good help.

racism. See Eduardo Bonilla-Silva, *Racism without Racists: Color-Blind Racism and the Persistence of Racial Inequality in America*, 4th ed. (Lanham, MD: Rowman & Littlefield, 2014), 25–52.

8. For a succinct account of Luther's views of sin, see L'ubomír Batka, "Martin Luther's Teaching on Sin," in *The Oxford Handbook of Martin Luther's Theology*, ed. Robert Kolb, Irene Dingel, and L'ubomír Batka (Oxford: Oxford University Press, 2014).

9. LW 13:149, 159.

Scanning the lives of nobles recorded in the pages of history, one quickly recognizes

> not only their unwillingness but also their incompetence for this. For the nobility at court and elsewhere corrupt themselves from youth on with carousing, playing, and peasant excesses. They grow up undisciplined, unbridled, inexperienced, and self-willed. This is why the nobility produces so few competent men, especially in the wine-lands. . . . It has often grieved me to see what fine fellows there were among the young nobility, well built in body and soul, like beautiful young saplings. And because there was no gardener to train them and to take care of them, they were uprooted by the swine, were left in their sap, and withered.[10]

Why is such wantonness so prevalent? Why are there so many swine, vicious people fattening themselves at royal troughs? Luther believes that the source of the problems lies in the sinful and corrupt nature of human beings because we "cannot stand to use honor, power, and authority in a Divine way."[11] This is Luther's general assessment of the human condition. But within the political realm, where worldly goods are had in great quantities, there one finds greater temptations and more abuses. "Aye, where else should such a little weed grow except in governments, where there is great power, honor, wealth, and friendship?"[12]

Poor leadership is a serious problem, and from Luther's perspective, this means that a ruler must guide and correct his or her officials. If a subordinate is openly practicing injustice, and the ruler does not correct this person, then the people will "pay more attention to his court and to his personnel and officials than to his orders; they follow the example of his household more than his own bidding, and they excuse themselves by contrasting his example with his own commandment."[13]

We see in Luther a strong emphasis on the ruler and the general conditions of life within a community. Evil and vice are dangerous, and indeed for Luther they are easier to practice and more prevalent than goodness and virtue. Uprooting vice once it has spread is a nearly impossible task. The devil readily exploits our weakness making it "difficult and laborious to remain steadfast."[14] The ruler must be diligent and check vice in his or her lands. As Luther puts it,

> If one permits a vice to spread and to become a habit, then there is no remedy. As Seneca says: "There is no room for a cure when what was vice

10. LW 13:215–16.
11. LW 13:212.
12. LW 13:208.
13. LW 13:170.
14. LW 13:215–16; WA 51:256.21–257.4.

becomes a habit. If vices become our habit, then it is all over." And the poet Ovid says very well: "Resist the beginnings. Check the evil when it begins; for once it gains the upper hand, help will come too slowly."[15]

Even though Luther is writing about the vices and evils of the sixteenth century, his trenchant analysis remains powerful and applicable today, especially as we consider the dangers of racism. Luther thinks that sin will flourish in places of wealth and prosperity, where there are economic incentives to continue sinning. Here we see the transition from individual sins to the formation of habits of sinning, or vices. Similarly, where racist systems offer deep psychological or economic benefits, we will find individuals motivated to keep these systems running. If left unchecked, Luther thinks that vice can spread and take root quickly, and so we ought not be surprised that racism is spread far and wide in our society given the five-hundred-year history of slavery, Jim Crow, and systematic discrimination at work in the Americas.

THE STORIES WE TELL: FORMATION THROUGH BAPTISM AND CONFESSION

Lest we believe ourselves to be helpless in uprooting racism from our lives and our institutions, let us now turn to some of Luther's helpful theological resources. Before we explore Luther's thinking, however, we might initially question whether he is a useful resource for addressing racism today. There are at least three reasons for this worry.

First, Luther lived and wrote at a time that many would say preceded the construction of racism as we know it today. The idea of discrete "races," each possessing predetermined traits, emerged from the confluence of particular ways of thought within the Western scientific community coupled with the rising institution of chattel slavery in the Americas. Luther, then, does not directly address race or racism, as these ideas and phenomena postdate him.

Second, while Luther did not possess the concepts of "race" or "ethnicity" as we understand them today, he did frequently make sweeping generalizations about large groups of people in ways that seem to equate group membership with specific moral failings. For example, the Swiss display a "mercenary spirit," while Luther laments the spread in Germany of "Italian virtues," which he describes as a love for fine, soft clothing and other luxury goods. But Luther's comments here can be

---

15. LW 13:222. See also LW 13:17, where Luther says that the average person "cannot set a wicked servant or housemaid right."

read as more innocuous, especially given his tendency to speak similarly about his own people and their problems with usury and drunkenness.[16]

Finally, we must acknowledge that Luther has a mixed record concerning questions of domination within the political realm. Nowhere is this more evident than in his response to the German Peasants' War of 1524–25. When some of the peasants called for an end to the institution of serfdom, arguing that a person freed in Christ ought not be the property of another, Luther disagreed. But not only did Luther reject their evangelical appeals for earthly freedom, he went so far as to say that a world where there were no serfs—or, we might say, slaves—is a world in chaos. Because of his limited political imagination, Luther could not envision a world free from hierarchical domination.[17] This final criticism of Luther cannot be ignored, but it can be overcome by extending Luther's insights into our role-specific responsibilities in ways that he himself was unable to do.

Moving from the critical to the constructive, we can examine Luther's theology of baptism. In his 1528 work *Concerning Rebaptism*, Luther's immediate concern is the growth of Anabaptist communities and their denial of infant baptism as a legitimate Christian practice.[18] Instead of revisiting debates about the relative merits of infant versus adult baptism, I want to draw our attention to two ways Luther discusses identity and certainty in the tract. The first concerns how baptism poses a threat to *the myths on which we rely*, and the second on how baptism serves as a reminder of *the people on whom we rely*.

Luther begins his defense of infant baptism by defending his own rejection of the papacy while also acknowledging his deep dependency on the Roman Church and the larger Western Christian tradition. As Luther reads them, his opponents miss the complex relationship in which we stand to those who came before us. Yes, certain aspects of the church's past must be challenged and even rejected, but this does not

---

16. LW 13:222. A certain form of nationalistic pride was an important contributor to the rise of the Reformations in Europe. As Heiko Oberman puts it, "Luther considered himself a German; and the German patriotic movement, which was just then beginning to move beyond mere protest against Roman influence and papal exploitation, bid with high hopes for his favor. Indeed, the sixteenth century saw the first signs of a national consciousness. . . . The connection between the Reformation and national consciousness may not be overlooked." See Heiko Oberman, "The Nationalist Conscription of Martin Luther," in *Piety, Politics, and Ethics: Reformation Studies in Honor of George Wolfgang Forell*, ed. Carter Lindberg (Kirksville, MO: Northeast Missouri State University Press, 1984), 66.

17. See Luther's *Admonition to Peace: A Reply to the Twelve Articles of the Peasants of Swabia*, LW 46:3–45. For more on this topic, see my "Reconciling Rapacious Wolves and Misguided Sheep: Law and Responsibility in Martin Luther's Response to the German Peasant's War," *Political Theology* 19, no. 4 (2018): 264–81.

18. Martin Luther, *Concerning Rebaptism*, LW 40:229–62.

require a wholesale rejection of traditions and history. This would deny the good that we have received and could lead us to the egregious conclusion that we simply create ourselves out of nothing. To proceed in this way "we would have to disown the whole of Scripture and the office of the ministry. . . . We on our part confess that there is much that is Christian and good under the papacy; indeed everything that is Christian and good is to be found there and has come to us from this source."[19] In this criticism of self-creation, a claim that would seek to denigrate or deny traditions, we see Luther's persistent suspicion about the stories we tell ourselves about ourselves. As sinful creatures, we are prone to indulge in self-promotion. The theology of baptism, then, offers an important corrective to this persistent temptation.

Building on this appeal to history and tradition, Luther engages in a long, rhetorical argument about the certainty of our faith. His opponents, Luther thinks, demand that we have certainty of our faith and argue that this is not possible if our baptism and faith are received in our infancy. How do I *know* that I came to believe, or was even capable of belief, as a baby? Luther embarks on a kind of *reductio* that asks how we could possibly sustain this kind of skepticism, rejecting everything that we have not seen or tested for ourselves. Going down this road would lead us to question other things, such as whether our so-called parents are who they say they are. "My friend," Luther asks,

> how do you know that this man is your father and this woman your mother? You cannot trust people, you must be sure of your own birth. . . . Likewise I might refuse to recognize anyone as my brother, sister, cousin, or relative, constantly repeating "I did not know we were related, because I am uncertain who my parents were." . . . To be among such Christians would be no better than being among wild wolves.[20]

Living as he did in a time before Maury Povich and DNA cheek swabs, Luther suggests that you have several ways of knowing that those familiar adults are indeed your parents. One source of assurance comes from the fact that these are the people who have cared for you. You cannot deny that these people have provided you with a home, clothing, food, and care throughout your life. This alone should make you believe that they are your family.

But, added to this evidence and, indeed, more important for Luther is the fact that others have borne witness to you that this is indeed your family. You don't know that these are your parents because you witnessed your own birth and childhood, but because others bear witness

19. LW 40:231.
20. LW 40:234.

of this to and for you. The same pattern is repeated in our lives within the Christian family. In the church, "you are reckoned among Christians, admitted to the sacraments, and to the use of all Christian privileges." Luther even goes so far to say that one "is much more certain of his or her baptism through the witness of Christians than if he himself had witnessed," so that one "would have to fall back finally on the testimony of Christians to be at peace."[21] Ultimately you rely on the testimony of others to know yourself.

In his writings on the sacrament of baptism, Luther emphasizes the positive aspect of receiving your identity from others. But, of course, we know that the stories others tell us can be both liberating and oppressive, affirming our dignity or denigrating our humanity. One powerful example of this denigration along racialized lines is on display in the work of another Luther, Dr. Martin Luther King Jr.

King's "Letter from Birmingham Jail" is a powerful, Christian response to those white moderates who believe that the civil rights movement and direct action are "untimely." As King describes it these faithful men can only reach this faithless conclusion because of their safe and privileged positions. In contrast, black people "have waited more than three hundred and forty years for our God-given and constitutional rights," King says.[22] He is moved to speak now because of the times that racism and prejudice have condemned him to silence. Perhaps recalling an actual experience, King says,

> When you suddenly find your tongue twisted and your speech stammering as you seek to explain to your six-year-old daughter why she cannot go to the public amusement park that has just been advertised on television, and see the tears welling up in her little eyes when she is told that Funtown is closed to colored children, and see the depressing clouds of inferiority begin to form in her little mental sky, and see her begin to distort her little personality by unconsciously developing a bitterness toward white people . . . when you are harried by day and haunted by night by the fact that you are a Negro, living constantly at tiptoe stance, never quite knowing what to expect next, and plagued with inner fears and outer resentments; when you are forever fighting a degenerating sense of "nobodyness"—then you will understand why we find it difficult to wait.[23]

Returning to our German Reformer with King's powerful testimony before us, we can better appreciate the complicated relationship between stories and identities. Luther's theology declares our irreducible

21. LW 40:239.
22. Martin Luther King Jr., "Letter from Birmingham Jail," in *Why We Can't Wait* (Boston: Beacon, 2010), 91–92.
23. King, "Letter from Birmingham Jail," 92.

dependence on the stories we have received about ourselves, but it does not demand that we simply embrace everything we hear. No simple formula will tell us in advance which stories to receive and which ones we should reject. While Luther demands that our baptismal identity must always take priority over the other ways we identify ourselves, this does not predetermine what we do with the stories about our family and community, let alone the myriad of intersectional identities connected to race, ethnicity, gender, sexuality, and socioeconomic class. Put simply, Luther does not give us all the answers or do the work for us. Instead, I believe, he encourages us to see again how the stories, spoken aloud or enshrined in institutions, deeply shape how we view ourselves and make our way in the world.

Luther builds on this view of baptism and bearing witness in his theology of confession. Because the practice of confession was so embedded within the late-medieval theology of penance Luther rejected, debates ensued about what role confession might take in the theology coming from, and inspirited by, Luther and the Wittenberg Reformers.[24] Rather than retaining confession as a separate sacrament, Luther preferred to see confession and repentance as a means of continuing to live into the death and rebirth of baptism. As he says in the Large Catechism, "Repentance, therefore, is nothing else than a return and approach to baptism, to resume and practice what has earlier been begun but abandoned" and to "practice the work that makes us Christian."[25] This return is never abandoned but must be constant throughout one's life. To borrow Jonathan Trigg's phrasing, we ought to speak of baptism here in the "present tense," the ongoing effects of our encounter with God's Spirit that should be viewed as an ongoing spiral instead of a vicious circle in which we wallow in the same sins or a triumphant line of progress in which we imagine ourselves forever free.[26]

In Luther's writing we can see how confession and repentance take place within the church's worship life, but they also spill over into our lives with and for each other in the community. One place where we can notice this is in his exposition in the Large Catechism of the eighth

24. For a detailed account of early evangelical debates about the status and function of confession that focuses on the controversies surrounding Andreas Osiander in Nuremberg, Ronald K. Rittgers emphasizes the shift that Lutheran thought introduced, making detailed and exhaustive confession of individual wrongs unnecessary without thereby removing the importance of both personal and general confession. See Ronald K. Rittgers, *The Reformation of the Keys: Confession, Conscience, and Authority in Sixteenth-Century Germany* (Cambridge, MA: Harvard University Press, 2004).

25. See the Large Catechism, BC 466 and 401 respectively. For an account of how Luther's theology of confession and absolution fits within his understanding of law and gospel, see John T. Pless, "Confession and Absolution," *Lutheran Quarterly* 30 (2016): 28–42.

26. See Jonathan D. Trigg, *Baptism in the Theology of Martin Luther* (Leiden: Brill, 1994), 75.

commandment against bearing false witness. Because of the temptation to lie, particularly when there is a danger to be feared or some gain to be had, being honest requires a measure of boldness or fearlessness.[27]

Luther draws a distinction between private sins and public sins, recommending that we not expose the former and that we should instead consistently seek to see our neighbors in the best possible light. Applied to the challenge of racism, Luther's distinction between private and public sins might be deeply problematic. If we view racism purely as an internal state, having mistaken ideas or feelings, we might be inclined to read Luther as recommending that we gloss over racism as a minor indiscretion and a personal problem. But this reading of Luther would be mistaken for at least two different reasons. First, Luther's fears about digging into private sins are situated in such a way that we can see he clearly has more salacious gossip or slander in his sights. Luther warns against those who would speculate and spread damaging rumors about neighbors based on little to no evidence.[28] This is why Luther's views about authority and intention are important here. In attempting to ferret out our neighbors' vices, Luther believes we are taking on the role of judge and jury in order to tear others down while building ourselves up. While such questionable motives *might* be at play in a confrontation with racism, this does not mean that all such confrontations are necessarily this malicious or misguided.

Second, as I discussed above, it is mistaken to limit our definition of racism to internal dispositions. Racism is a complex phenomenon that involves both individual agents and larger institutions and structures. Within Luther's typology, then, racism would have to be categorized as a public sin. A public sin is one that can be known because it occurs in the light of day. In contrast to secret sins of the heart, a public sin like racism is witnessed by many. Racism is a sin committed in public that directly harms my neighbor.

As such, Luther's advice concerning public sins places an obligation on us to respond in such a way that "evil does not go unpunished."[29] Drawing on Matthew 18, Luther advises a series of small- and large-scale interventions, ranging from one-on-one encounters up to the

---

27. We might see in Luther a connection to ancient Greek thought about *parrhesia*, frank or bold speech. For more on Luther and the need for bold and truthful speech within church communities, see Reinhard Hütter, *Bound to Be Free: Evangelical Catholic Engagements in Ecclesiology, Ethics, and Ecumenism* (Grand Rapid: Eerdmans, 2004). Vitor Westhelle's work has drawn our attention to bold speech and liberatory struggles. See especially his *Transfiguring Luther: The Planetary Promise of Luther's Theology* (Eugene, OR: Cascade, 2016).

28. Large Catechism, BC 422.

29. Large Catechism, BC 422.

intervention of the whole community and its political leaders.[30] Applied to racism we can see how Luther's thought warrants not only confronting friends and family, but also calling on the civil authorities when appropriate. We can also recall Luther's comments on the fifth commandment, against killing, where he warns that we violate this not only by doing evil but also

> when we have the opportunity to do good to our neighbors and to prevent, protect, and save them from suffering bodily harm or injury, but fail to do so. . . . For you have withheld your love from them and robbed them of the kindness by means of which their lives might have been saved.[31]

In his theology and his practice, Luther called people to remember the importance of their baptismal identities. As we have seen, for him this involved several important moves. In baptism, we challenge the myth of self-creation and come to recognize the centrality of witness to and for one another. I am who I am, in part, because of the traditions that have shaped me. I come to know who I am in and through the stories that others share with me. Returning to my baptism requires confession and repentance, not just in private but in public spaces where sins rob and harm my neighbor. Applied to our efforts at confronting racism, we can leverage Luther's insights when coming to grips with our own dependence on others, the ways that racist stories distort identities, and the deep need for confrontation and change. Let us turn our attention from Luther's theology in its sixteenth-century context to a more modern public witness, James Baldwin.

JAMES BALDWIN AS EXEMPLAR

As I indicated above, racism as we know and experience it today did not yet exist in Luther's time. For this reason, and others, if we are going to confront racism in our world we will need resources beyond Luther's theology. One powerful resource is the work of the author and social critic James Baldwin. As we will see, Baldwin's thought embodies several of the themes I have identified in Luther's thought—the power of narratives to construct or deconstruct identity and the challenging work of confession in public.[32]

30. Large Catechism, BC 423.
31. Large Catechism, BC 412.
32. While I have already invoked Martin Luther King Jr., and making connections between the two Luthers would certainly be appropriate, I have chosen to engage Baldwin's thought because, in my opinion, Baldwin's words have not been anesthetized to the same extent the King's have. Let me be clear—I believe that Dr. King was and remains a radical and

Born in 1924, James Baldwin grew up in Harlem, New York, in the wake of the Harlem Renaissance. His stepfather, the only father he knew in his childhood, was a Baptist preacher. Baldwin himself spent at least three years as a preacher and minister in a storefront church in Harlem. While Baldwin grew to become a severe critic of Christianity, it is better to see these criticisms emerging from the life and experience of a man who left—but never abandoned—religiosity.[33] Indeed, we might be tempted to say that Baldwin, like Luther, took to heart the prophetic need to criticize a church because it had gone astray. Baldwin called out a church that constructed a white God, a God who claimed to love all while simultaneously casting down black people.[34] Through his criticism, Baldwin called the church to reckon with its history of encouraging self-hatred and being more concerned with souls than bodies.[35] Ultimately, Baldwin says, the "concept of God" must be pushed to expand, so that it "makes us larger, freer, and more loving. If God cannot do this, then it is time we got rid of Him."[36]

Across his writing, Baldwin often reflects on the enduring importance of his work and identity as a writer and artist. Much as Luther emphasized the importance of stories in the creation of our identities, Baldwin examines the way that those who craft stories bear a responsibility for deep examination and social critique. In a short article reflecting on the state of literature in the 1960s, Baldwin describes the novelist's task as "attempting to tell as much of the truth as one can bear, and then a little more." The writer engages in a kind of truth-telling that pushes people beyond their limits by exposing them to the truth. "It

confrontational figure, one whose deep criticisms of racism, poverty, and war still need to be heard today. But there is a tendency to assume that we "get" King, that we understand his project and sayings, in ways that make it difficult to see his sharp and cutting edges. For various reasons, Baldwin has not yet suffered this same fate.

33. Clifton L. Granby's recent dissertation argues that James Baldwin should be read as a prophetic exemplar of social criticism and love, whose insights draw on and can inspire Christian communities. See his "Fruits of Love: Self and Social Criticism in James Baldwin and Howard Thurman" (PhD diss., Princeton University, 2015). For an account of Baldwin's prophetic work in the realm of democratic theory more than religious studies, see Lawrie Balfour, *The Evidence of Things Not Said: James Baldwin and the Promise of American Democracy* (Ithaca, NY: Cornell University Press, 2001).

34. James Baldwin, "Down at the Cross: Letter from a Region of My Mind," in *The Fire Next Time* (New York: Dial Press, 1963), 45.

35. Baldwin, "Down at the Cross," 53, 59.

36. Baldwin, "Down at the Cross," 61. Sondra A. O'Neale says that in Baldwin, "The reality of that unseen spiritual truth, codified in his novels by the suffering blues and tarrying spiritual motifs, enables him to keep advocating that the demonstrable love of Christ will bring to earth that paradise revealed on the threshing floor and fulfill the prophecy in Amos 9:7, 'Are ye not as children of the Ethiopians unto me, O children of Israel?'" See her "Fathers, Gods, and Religion: Perceptions of Christianity and Ethnic Faith in James Baldwin," in *Critical Essays on James Baldwin*, ed. Fred L. Standley and Nancy V. Burt (Boston: G. K. Hall, 1988), 125–43, here 141.

is, alas, the truth that to be an American writer today means mounting an unending attack on all that Americans believe themselves to hold sacred. It means fighting an astute and agile guerrilla warfare with that American complacency which so inadequately masks the American panic."[37]

The work of unmasking is difficult work. Baldwin came to understand how difficult it could be as he reflected on his own identity as an American black man living abroad in Paris for much of his adult life. In his collection of essays *Nobody Knows My Name*, Baldwin says,

> This perpetual dealing with people very different from myself caused a shattering in me of preconceptions I scarcely knew I held. . . . This forces the writer to reconsider many things he had always taken for granted. This reassessment, which can be very painful, is also very valuable. This freedom, like all freedom, has its dangers and its responsibilities.[38]

Much like Luther, Baldwin appreciated the need to push against one's tradition without ever being able to fully disconnect from that tradition. Every person must be "born somewhere," Baldwin writes. "He may leave the group that produced him—he may be forced to—but nothing will efface his origins, the marks of which he carries with him everywhere."[39] Recognizing one's social location stands in Baldwin's thought as an invitation to take a critical stance toward one's people—the community, the church, and the nation, to name but a few. Here, we need the kind of boldness and honesty that Luther spoke of. As Baldwin puts it,

> The time has come, God knows, for us to examine ourselves, but we can only do this if we are willing to free ourselves from the myth of America and try to find out what is really happening here. Every society is really governed by hidden laws, but unspoken but profound assumptions on the part of the people, and ours is no exception. It is up to the American writer to find out what these laws and assumptions are.[40]

In his efforts to examine and expose the often-repeated myths and tacit laws at work in America, Baldwin teaches us to dig deeper into the causes and effects of racism. His patient observations of the forces at work provide us with opportunities to see our actions anew. In the

37. James Baldwin, "As Much Truth as One Can Bear," *New York Times*, January 14, 1962, 11.

38. James Baldwin, "The Discovery of What It Means to Be an American," in *Nobody Knows My Name*, in *James Baldwin: Collected Essays*, ed. Toni Morrison (New York: Library of America, 1998), 140–41.

39. Baldwin, "Nobody Knows My Name," 141.

40. Baldwin, "Nobody Knows My Name," 142.

early 1960s, Baldwin traveled alongside Dr. King as the civil rights leader preached and organized across the South. Baldwin takes this as an opportunity to reflect on racism, Dr. King's leadership qualities, and other issues within the civil rights movement.

As a Northerner traveling in the South, he is aware of the temptations faced by those above the Mason-Dixon line to see racism and segregation as Southern problems. Echoing perhaps Martin Luther's attacks on the sins of inactivity and things left undone, Baldwin makes clear that the North's complicity comes with culpability. All the injustice of slavery, segregation, and racism "could never have come about at all without the tacit consent of the North, and this consent robs the North, historically and actually, of any claim to moral superiority."[41]

Baldwin traveled in and around Montgomery after the desegregation of the public transit system had been enforced. Riding on a bus, he observes that the whites do not seem angry but instead are strangely silent. He attributes this silence to a deep sense of hurt and betrayal:

> They had been betrayed by the Negroes, not merely because the Negros had declined to remain in their "place," but because the Negroes had refused to be controlled by the town's image of them. And, without this image, it seemed to me, the whites were abruptly and totally lost. The very foundations of their private and public worlds were being destroyed.[42]

Again, Baldwin is keenly aware of the power that myths and images have, how the narratives we tell ourselves can control our view of the world, and how bitter and resentful we can become when these stories are shaken.

When discussing leadership in the black community, Baldwin notes that previous leaders, such as Booker T. Washington, were often forced to work within the strictures of the racist power structure. While Washington may or may not have really thought that segregation was a good policy for blacks in America,

> he *did* know that he could accomplish his objective by telling white men what they wanted to hear. And it has never been very difficult for a Negro in this country to figure out what white men want to hear: he takes his condition as an echo of their desires.[43]

---

41. James Baldwin, "The Dangerous Road before Martin Luther King," in *Collected Essays*, 640.

42. Baldwin, "The Dangerous Road," 642.

43. Baldwin, "The Dangerous Road," 640.

Washington represents the kind of struggle that many black leaders, and black people more broadly, faced. This is the struggle to achieve power and recognition before whites while simultaneously remaining connected to, and advocating for, the black community. What Baldwin respects about Dr. King is the way that he seems to have managed this tension through love. He does not just say what people in power want to hear, and he does not sink into the kind of despair and resentment that can plague leaders of social movements. As Baldwin sees it, "the fact that King really loves the people he represents" prevents him from hating either his people or the white people who oppose him.[44]

As I noted above, Baldwin remained indebted to the African American Pentecostal religiosity he was steeped in during his childhood in Harlem. To the best of my knowledge Baldwin never directly engaged the work of Martin Luther. That said, Baldwin did recognize and respect something about the Lutheran tradition as represented in the work of the famous Swedish director Ingmar Bergman. While living and traveling in Europe, Baldwin was presented with an opportunity to interview Bergman and described the encounter in an essay, "The Northern Protestant."[45] Baldwin is struck by Bergman's style and the religious sensibility in his films. "I thought," Baldwin says, "how there was something in the weird, mad, Northern Protestantism which reminded me of the visions of the black preachers of my childhood."[46] Baldwin specifically appreciates how in Bergman's film The Seventh Seal, the human being finds strength in weakness, how he "outwits death by opposing to this anonymous force his weak and ineradicable humanity."[47]

44. Baldwin, "The Dangerous Road," 639. Cornel West has written a great deal about the importance of love in James Baldwin's work of prophetic social criticism. As he puts it, "For Baldwin, the seemingly impossible flight from white supremacy takes the form of a Chekhovian effort to endure lovingly and compassionately, guided by a vision of freedom and empowered by a tradition of black love and faith. To be a bastard people—wrenched from Africa and in, but never fully of, America—is to be a people of highly limited options, if any at all. To bear witness is to make and remake, invent and reinvent oneself as a person and people by keeping faith with the best of such earlier efforts, yet also to acknowledge that the very new selves and peoples to emerge will never fully find a space, place, or face in American society—or Africa. This perennial process of self-making and self-inventing is propelled by a self-loving and self-trusting made possible by overcoming a colonized mind, body, and soul." See West's essay "Black Strivings in a Twilight Civilization," in The Cornel West Reader (New York: Basic Civitas Books, 1999), 107.

45. James Baldwin, "The Northern Protestant," in Collected Essays, 244.

46. Baldwin, "The Northern Protestant," 244.

47. Baldwin, "The Northern Protestant," 243.

Baldwin is clearly impressed with the complicated view of the heroic and the tragic in Bergman's characters. Reflecting on this he wonders if he might be able to turn his own bitterness into a force for good if he imagines himself as a kind of tragic hero, levering the complexity of his own life and strife in new ways. He describes this turn using the language of confession and honesty:

> All art is a kind of confession, more or less oblique. All artists, if they are to survive, are forced, at last, to tell the whole story, to vomit the anguish up. All of it, the literal and the fanciful. Bergman's authority seemed, then, to come from the fact that he was reconciled to this arduous, delicate, and disciplined self-exposure.[48]

I can think of no better words than Baldwin's for describing what the work of genuine Christians, who happen to be Lutherans or "Northern Protestants," might look like—this drive to tell as much of the truth as one can bear, and then a bit more, packaged in confession as self-exposure. Bringing Luther and Baldwin together allows us to see both theological weight and social power in the work of bearing witness to the sin of racism in the United States.

PRACTICAL SUGGESTIONS FOR CONGREGATIONS TODAY

While these insights and comparisons between Martin Luther and James Baldwin are instructive, to make them concrete we must consider how congregations might embody and enact the legacies of Luther and Baldwin today. Every congregation finds itself in a unique situation, and so I offer these suggestions with an eye toward what I see as common problems in many of the predominately white Lutheran congregations I have seen, served, and worshiped with.

First, I believe that we should avoid bland appeals to baptism that make it some past event that establishes our equality before God and one another. It remains true today, as it was in Paul's ministry among Romans and Galatians, that all stand equally before God as sinners and as one in Christ Jesus (Rom 3:23; Gal 3:28). But there are several problems with this understanding of baptism and the effect this kind of thinking has in the face of the challenges of racism. As we saw above, Luther defended the view that baptism is secured in the past but must be experienced and lived in the present. Furthermore, while baptism does establish our equal standing before God, we are all too aware of the

48. Baldwin, "The Northern Protestant," 246.

real inequalities we experience in our lives before one another. I would chasten us to avoid making baptism the theological equivalent of "All Lives Matter." Whatever the motivations for such an appeal, it has the effect of erasing, or even denying, inequality and injustice. If Luther can teach us anything, it is that we need to confess our real sins and attend to our neighbors' real needs, neither of which can happen if we believe that every instance of sin and every claim for help is the same. What Baldwin, King, and others teach us is that the claims to equality enshrined in our theological and civic values stand before us as law—as judgments that call us to repent for our repeated failures.

Building on this, I suggest that congregations and their leaders would do well to name specific and particular instances of racism as sin in our midst. One problem I have observed is the tendency to avoid taking on racism directly by making oblique and passing references to issues in the world today. I suspect that pastors who make occasional references to #BlackLivesMatter, the shooting of Michael Brown in Ferguson, or other current events are well-meaning, striving to recognize the connection between the pulpit and the world. But I also suspect that a passing comment does more to tick a box and assuage our guilt than it actually does to address the issues. Instead of scattering litanies of racial sins across a handful of sermons, I would challenge congregational leaders to take on racism in entire sermons and educational opportunities.

While pastors can be at the forefront of this work, they can also become complacent or resistant to such efforts. It is therefore the responsibility of all people to educate themselves and others about the depth and complexity of the issues surrounding racism in America today. If we are not pushing ourselves to tell more truth than we can bear, then we are not being witnesses to the God who bore the sins of the world. Be concrete and particular, for as Baldwin puts it, we must "utilize the particular in order to reveal something much larger and heavier than any particular can be."[49] In Luther's language, we might say that the finite can bear the infinite, that God comes clothed in the mundane, and so it is here that we must encounter God. Applied to racism, then, linger on the good and the difficult that we might see in the #BlackLivesMatter movement instead of simply acknowledging that it exists.

Finally, to confront racism in ourselves requires confronting racist structures and institutions. We must move beyond inculcating antiracist feelings and thoughts in our members and toward constructing antiracist systems in our congregations and throughout local and national governments. Keeping our conversations as concrete and specific as

49. Baldwin, "As Much Truth," 11.

possible is vitally important here. Look at how discriminatory housing practices established the neighborhood in which your church sits. Instead of just blessing the seniors who graduate each spring, invite conversation about the inequalities in educational and employment opportunities that exist in your city or town. Continue to press your sisters and brothers in Christ in places where deeply personal conversations are supposed to emerge—coffee-hour reflections, lugging around crafts and costumes for VBS, or the quiet moments before choir rehearsals. We must own and take responsibility for the failure among Lutheran congregations to adequately reflect the rich racial and ethnic diversity that surrounds us. All of this can be hard for us to do, in part because the work of discerning the best policy action is extremely difficult and, in part, because many Lutherans have traditionally found vocal public engagement and confrontation off-putting. But I know of one Lutheran who overcame the temptations of reticence and quietism quite successfully. His name was Martin Luther.

In his *Commentary on Psalm 101*, which I mentioned above, Luther offers a mirror to instruct Elector John Frederick and others in the ways of right leadership. Partway through the commentary, Luther pauses and anticipates an objection to his approach. Luther has repeatedly insisted that the spiritual and temporal kingdoms must remain distinct, a position often referred to as the two kingdoms doctrine or teaching. And so, Luther imagines his readers complaining that Luther himself seems to be mixing up these kingdoms with his extended advice on how rulers should govern the land. Luther is somewhat dismissive of this objection, because he suspects it is motivated by a desire to silence Luther rather than a genuine desire to respect the sovereignty of the political realm. Often those who tell you to "wait," or warn that you are being transgressive, really just want you to quiet down so the status quo can continue unabated. Nevertheless, Luther replies to this criticism by saying that the one who demands improvements in the government is not "meddling." "On the contrary," Luther says, this one "is thereby serving and being obedient to the highest government." The church, as church, has no right to take over the government in a "dictatorial and dominating fashion," but it does have an obligation to call out sin and demand more.[50] Christians can recognize injustice, call out inept political leadership, and insist that a vice like racism be rooted out of both individual hearts and the sinuous structures of the political body.

Martin Luther and James Baldwin both loved people enough to challenge them. They opened the eyes of their people to their sins, forcing them to see the lies at work. But they also laid themselves open

50. LW 13:195–96.

to their people, inviting conversations and controversy. If congregations are to become places where racism is addressed, in real and concrete ways, that we must follow the example set by these forebears. Remembering Luther five hundred years after the Reformation involves more than just returning to his texts. It also involves living a life that keeps Luther's legacy alive today.

6.

God's Word Spoken Publicly, Boldly, and Honestly

AMY REUMANN

The Forgotten Luther: Reclaiming the Social-Economic Dimension of the Reformation uncovered the rich resources on poverty, wealth, and Christian responsibility that Martin Luther left for us to explore in our own time. After its publication, Bishop Tracie Bartholomew of the Evangelical Lutheran Church in America's (ELCA's) New Jersey Synod ordered 175 copies of the book for all the congregations in her state. The synod offered workshops led by Pastor Sara Lilja, director of Lutheran Episcopal Advocacy Ministry New Jersey, to equip congregations to lead local discussions on economic injustice. Pastor Lilja said, "We were thrilled to see over 300 persons attend the workshops. We had to order more books and deliver them after the assembly!"

Community reading, learning, and immersion experience around a theological book is not unusual. But engaging hundreds of people who represent the entire spectrum of political affiliations and theological perspectives around a discussion of economics, income disparity, and the role of the church in public life is decidedly rare. And risky. Many congregations already face enough friction in their life together without looking for more, particularly in the fraught arenas of public policy and politics.

Hunger for the kind of discussion that took place among New Jersey Lutherans was echoed in Lutheran churches around the country, even as the 2016 presidential campaigns were heating up, Congress grew more polarized along ideological lines, and families and congregations experienced the strain of heightened incivility and heated rhetoric. As the essays in this volume show, Luther lived and taught a living and lively faith that inspires and enables us to respond to God's grace by moving us from our private lives into the public square for the well-being of our neighbor. It offers a powerful corrective to an individualistic American understanding of liberty that is often reduced to freedom as an end in itself. Luther's understanding of freedom is grounded in God's grace, which frees us from sin and for service to promote the well-being of our neighbor and the wholeness of communities. We are not the final recipient of God's grace; our neighbor is, through our public word and deeds. And when needed, the church is to speak out, show up, protest if necessary, in a visible expression of neighbor love.

This focus on loving our neighbor is not the image most US Lutherans have of their church. The denominational snapshot Carter Lindberg offers in his essay—a football team in a huddle with only their backsides showing—is not too far from the public perception of Lutherans as a denomination that keeps a low profile on the American religious scene. It is also the view many Lutherans have of themselves, counting a focus on internal matters and quietism toward the issues of the day as the proper relationship of church to world.

Rightly remembering Luther and a Reformation worthy of the name will not let us remain in that place. The purpose of a football huddle is not to stay there, but to exchange information and agree on your next moves so you can go back on the field to accomplish your mission. The church in the world, too, comes together to hear God's Word, share bread and wine, and experience God's amazing grace and then is drawn by the Holy Spirit to break the huddle and head back out to be a church for the world.

The church responds to human need in a variety of ways. First and important steps are prayer and financial giving alongside dedicated ministries of service: feeding the hungry, sheltering the homeless, and providing community health services or education, all of which demonstrate our Lutheran care for others. Some congregations add ministries of justice to this list. The concerns raised in these chapters—dismantling systemic racism, promoting reconciliation, upholding human dignity, honoring the well-being of bodies, promoting education, ensuring health care for everyone—are all places where the public voice and leadership of the church make a difference. Churches make change through community organizing and economic development ministries, as well as public policy change through ministries of advocacy. These ministries are key ways we can move out of the huddle and onto the field, as a church for the sake of the world.

FROM LUTHER'S CATECHISM TO SOCIAL STATEMENTS

Faith active in the world builds on Luther's understanding that God's reign in the world includes working through the governing structures. Government, he taught, is a gift from God for order, peace, and caring for one's neighbor.[1] Lutherans don't have a stake in any one form of government, as long as it is fulfilling several key functions, such as ensuring sufficiency for all and maintaining peace and order. In the Large Catechism, Luther addresses the role of government three times, with an emphasis on the ways God acts through it to care for the most vulnerable:

- Fourth Commandment: Civil government is an extension of the responsibility and authority of the parental role and is to serve society, so that all people have their basic needs met and can live full and productive lives.[2]

- First Article of the Apostles' Creed: Good government is a gift of God and a blessing alongside necessities such as body, soul, life, nourishment, air, water, peace, and security.[3]

- Fourth Petition of the Lord's Prayer: Daily bread includes all we need for our daily life, and the role of rulers is to ensure daily bread for all.[4]

Luther stressed the essential role of government as a means by which God cares for the most vulnerable. In his commentary on Psalm 82, he addressed the princes who further the Word of God by ensuring "justice for those who fear God," including establishing laws to prevent the oppression of "the poor, the wretched, widows and orphans." The government, he said, is a "divine hospital" that cares for the poor, widows, and orphans and ensures no one will become a beggar.

Christians are to cooperate with, participate in, and submit to the just laws of a benevolent government that prioritizes the physical and economic well-being of the people, with special consideration for the needs of the those who are poor or vulnerable to exploitation. But submission to the governing authorities is never blind or automatic. We are to evaluate laws, discuss policies as a faith community, and discern a faithful response. In my denomination, the ELCA, we do so within the framework and with guidance of our social teaching documents, which

1. The Augsburg Confession 16, On Civil Authority, BC 49–50.
2. The Large Catechism, BC 407.
3. The Apostles' Creed, BC 432–33.
4. The Lord's Prayer, BC 450.

are grounded in an understanding of how God can and does work in the world through the governing authorities for the common good, while holding them to account when they do not reflect that higher purpose.

The first of these documents, *The Church in Society: A Lutheran Perspective*, provides the foundation for this work. It affirms that the witness of the church in society is rooted in "identity as a community that lives from and for the Gospel. . . . It is in grateful response to God's grace in Jesus Christ that this church carries out its responsibility for the well-being of society and the environment."[5] Our actions, our voice, our advocacy begin in God's justifying action in our lives, which then flows through us into care for our communities. At the same time, the church "must participate in social structures critically, for sin also is at work in the world. . . . This church, therefore, must unite realism and vision, wisdom and courage, in its social responsibility. It needs constantly to discern when to support and when to confront society's cultural patterns, values, and powers."[6]

The ELCA develops social teaching documents and messages built on a Lutheran understanding of Scripture, the theology of the Lutheran Confessions, and the experience of Lutheran ministries. These documents guide reflection, discussion, and action in the public realm. Social statements provide broad frameworks to assist us in thinking about and discussing social issues in the context of faith and life. They are created in a process of prayer, study of an issue with experts in the field, and theological discernment, with invitations for discussion and input from congregations. Passing a social statement at churchwide assembly is not the goal. It is just the beginning. Once passed, these living documents provide a framework for witnessing as an institution and a foundation for advocacy of the church to address hunger, poverty, care for environment, peace in our world, racism, and a host of other concerns.

Many of the ELCA social statements and social messages (documents passed by the ELCA Church Council that expand on individual topics) originate when individuals or congregations look for guidance on issues that affect them or their communities. For example, when a scientist who worked in the field of genetics asked his pastor what the church had to say about his vocation, they were unable to identify any sources. This question eventually resulted in several years of discussion and discernment, and development of the social statement *Genetics, Faith and Responsibility*.

5. Evangelical Lutheran Church in America, *Church in Society: A Lutheran Perspective* (Chicago: ELCA, 1991), 1–2.

6. ELCA, *Church in Society*, 3.

Reactions to ELCA social teaching can range from appreciation to rejection. Some people are delighted to discover teaching documents that faithfully examine issues of concern and offer guidance for decision making. Others may respond by saying, "This doesn't speak for me" or "I didn't vote on this" when they engage with a statement. ELCA social teachings are not intended to speak for all Lutherans at all times. They do not have the authority to dictate thoughts or actions. But they do provide a starting point (and study guides) to bring Lutherans together in the practice of faithful discernment and discussion on issues that affect the church and the world. Social teaching documents also serve as a guide to our institution's advocacy on public policy, particularly through "Implementing Resolutions" sections that appear at the end of each document and give specific directives for advocacy work.

God acts through those who govern in the pursuit of greater justice. We are to pray for and support their vocation. We are also called to strenuously oppose policies that deny justice and even to actively resist, if necessary. The *Church in Society* social statement spells this out:

> As a prophetic presence, this church has the obligation to name and denounce the idols before which people bow, to identify the power of sin present in social structures, and to advocate in hope with poor and powerless people. When religious or secular structures, ideologies, or authorities claim to be absolute, this church says, "We must obey God rather than any human authority" (Acts 5:29). With Martin Luther, this church understands that "to rebuke" those in authority "through God's Word spoken publicly, boldly and honestly" is "not seditious" but "a praiseworthy, noble and . . . particularly great service to God."[7]

GOD'S WORD SPOKEN PUBLICLY, BOLDLY, AND HONESTLY

The Statement of Purpose in the ELCA constitution includes several clear directives for the role of the church in society, including the following:

- Serve in response to God's love to meet human needs, caring for the sick and the aged, advocating dignity and justice for all people, working for peace and reconciliation among the nations, and standing with the poor and powerless and committing itself to their needs.[8]

7. ELCA, *The Church in Society*, 4.
8. ELCA, *Constitution, Bylaws, and Continuing Resolutions of the Evangelical Lutheran Church in*

- Lift its voice in concord and work in concert with forces for good, to serve humanity, cooperating with church and other groups participating in activities that promote justice, relieve misery, and reconcile the estranged.

- Study social issues and trends, work to discover the causes of oppression and injustice, and develop programs of ministry and advocacy to further human dignity, freedom, justice, and peace in the world.

- Work with civil authorities in areas of mutual endeavor, maintaining institutional separation of church and state in a relation of functional interaction.[9]

This purpose is built squarely on the foundation of Luther's careful connection between a church that serves and a church that speaks. As an institution, the ELCA currently works in four distinct arenas where the church can build on ministries of service through speaking to public issues:

- ELCA Advocacy in Washington, DC, helps facilitate the national network of ELCA members advocating on federal policy issues that affect vulnerable people and God's creation.

- The Lutheran Office for World Community monitors the work of the United Nations on behalf of the ELCA and the Lutheran World Federation, working for peace, dignity, and reconciliation for all people.

- State Public Policy Offices provide a Lutheran advocacy presence at the state-government level, equipping congregations for advocacy ministry. Unique among denominations, this network of state offices is supported by ELCA World Hunger and speaks to the biblical values of hospitality to strangers, care for creation, and concern for people living in poverty and struggling with hunger and disease.

- Corporate Social Responsibility ministry addresses the social impact of corporations and their practices and governance by developing investment screens and engaging in shareholder advocacy and dialogue with company representatives, boards, and executives.

America (Chicago: ELCA, 1987), 4.02.c.
  9. *ELCA Constitution* 4.03.g.l.n.

The thread that runs through the four ELCA advocacy ministries is the church's commitment to God's vision of a just world where all are fed. It embodies our core concern for people who live at risk of hunger in a world where there is enough food but where people still suffer from malnutrition and famine and struggle to feed their families. The lion's share of this work is done as direct service that ensures food and aid are provided where they are needed, domestically and globally. But ELCA World Hunger's comprehensive approach shapes work carried out by many ELCA divisions and incorporates other tactics, including economic development, community organizing for grassroots-led systemic change, education on root causes of hunger, and public-policy advocacy. Together, these constitute a well-stocked toolbox to ensure Lutherans are using the many resources at their disposal.

The ELCA has professional policy staff in Washington, DC, and several state capitals who help facilitate Lutheran advocacy efforts through providing educational resources on current issues, defining policy priorities for the church, and sending out notices of action opportunities. But their presence on Capitol Hill or in state capitals is not enough. Elected lawmakers want to hear from their constituents. By communicating personal stories and experiences with their lawmakers and inviting them to visit their ministries and building relationships with them, congregations can make an impact on lawmakers' decisions. I sometimes hear from Lutherans who say it is no use reaching out to their lawmaker because "they never vote my way." It is always worth communicating! At the very least it ensures your representatives cannot claim constituents haven't spoken to them on a particular matter. Your voice will make sure elected leaders are better informed about their own districts when they deliberate and cast their votes. Faith-based advocates provide vital input that help lawmakers reach decisions on matters of moral importance.

Luther replaced the priest-centered model of church in his day with the priesthood of all believers. All persons through baptism are equipped to approach and serve God without intermediaries. Advocacy, too, requires leaders acting on their baptismal identity, testifying to their understanding of God's call to do justice, standing in solidarity with neighbors for healing and wholeness in their communities. Advocacy is a powerful way in which the church can create change by engaging lawmakers and government leaders to influence policy development and implementation. Our staff provide guidance and expertise, but the most important advocacy is the emails, letters, visits, and phone calls made by Lutherans around the country, every day.

A CHURCH EMPOWERED TO SPEAK

A frequent objection to advocacy by churches that I hear is the fear that it will divide the congregation. As a pastor who hesitated bringing conversation about social issues into the congregation said to me, "We can't agree on the color of the carpet in the nave, so how can we possibly talk about politics?" But *not* talking about politics is also not possible. Politics, from the Latin word for "city," is about our life together, what we hold in common, and how we care for one another as a community.

Those who would stay quiet rather than speak out must consider that saying nothing is also saying something. When the church chooses to not speak up to counter hunger, poverty, the desecration of creation, the sin of racism, or the denial of civil rights, it suggests that these things are okay and that the church is content with the status quo. The silence of Christians has been used to justify some of the most horrific crimes of humanity. Rather than shying from the cost of addressing an issue, we must also measure the cost of not speaking—the cost to our neighbor as well as the integrity of the church's witness to the gospel.

Before we act together as people of God, we have to talk together first. In a society where people are increasingly segregated by political affiliation, self-selecting into ideological silos, congregations offer one of the few places where people of diverse outlooks and opinions still regularly come together. While this diversity is sometimes seen as an obstacle to overcome, it can also be a source of strength. The apostle Paul wrote to deeply divided churches in his day, saying that, reconciled through Christ, they were freed to address their differences in a spirit of love, forgiveness, and unity. So are we. Congregational practices of worshiping and sharing the sacraments, joining in prayer, and studying Scripture together provide a foundation connecting people across political differences and partisan divides. The church can offer spaces and resources for living in the tension of our differences and, engaging in communal discernment, on the foundation of God's grace.

Congregations can develop their public voice by convening individuals and groups in their community for learning and action. Faith communities routinely open their doors to local groups and assemblies, providing a known and trusted space for their neighbors. But they can go further. Community institutions are usually willing to open their doors to local faith leaders who want to discuss community concerns. Civic, business, and other leaders readily accept invitations to meet with the congregation, to share challenges, and to shape vision for our common life. We can be conveners of conversations where diverse viewpoints can be shared and a way forward that will benefit an entire community can be sought.

Getting involved in issues in the public square helps the church to be the church. The church does not speak up to protect the institution or to advance its narrow self-interest. The model in Lutheran social teaching is that the church acts in public for the well-being of the whole society. When we begin to attend as a community to public issues, we exercise faith practices that embody our understanding of the gospel, witness to the world our public commitments, and communicate a different way of being a church. In every church I have served, public witness and advocacy have grown the congregation and brought new members attracted by that vision. Four of these practices are accompaniment, moving from mercy to justice, interreligious commitment, and public testimony.

Practice of Accompaniment

One state public policy office was arranging to bring people to the state capitol for a rally and lobby day on raising the minimum wage. We wanted to feature the testimony of the people who were most affected by the current wage to speak about the difference that an increase in income would make for them. But the people on our short list for speakers who earned minimum wage all had to decline the invitation, because they did not have the luxury to take time off, even for an event that would have such a direct impact on their future well-being.

A frequent saying about advocacy is that it is "a voice for the voiceless." The expression captures the Latin etymology of the root *advocare*, "to call to the aid of another." But the assumption behind this saying is that those most affected are unable to speak for themselves, a notion that needs to be challenged.

Accompaniment is a core concept in ELCA global mission, replacing former missionary models of doing for others with the image of learning to walk with our partners and support their priorities. Advocates need to learn accompaniment too. The content of our advocacy is changed when those most affected are part of defining, shaping, and delivering the message. I know a pastor who frequently visited his state capitol to address poverty issues. When the congregation rallied around a woman who was sleeping in the church parking lot, helping her back on her feet, the pastor invited her to attend a Lutheran lobby day on state budget cuts to antipoverty programs. During the visits, she shared her story of abuse and homelessness and then described what policy would be most helpful for women in her situation. The pastor's first inclination had been to tell her story in his own visits. The message was so much more powerful, he said, when he stepped back and she advocated for herself. How many of our ministries of service could invite and support those seeking assistance to also learn how to tell their story and speak to the policies that affect their lives? Our advocacy ministries would be deepened when our practice includes acting as conduits for the voices of people most affected.

The mere doing of advocacy can be a privilege. Online advocacy requires access to the internet and a permanent address to even participate in most systems. Attending advocacy or faith lobby events requires the financial means and time to travel to a state capital or Washington, DC. Disability-rights advocates once flooded the Pennsylvania state capitol but found some offices were inaccessible to the wheelchairs many of them used. Sometimes our efforts are best used to remove barriers by providing support, transportation, or funding for those who have experienced poverty, pollution, health concerns, or other matters, so they can speak for themselves.

Faith-based advocacy can be enhanced by using organizing practices that give priority to identifying and developing local leaders. Congregational outreach ministries are full of local leaders who can be a part of defining and speaking to their own issues and solutions, rather than having anyone, no matter how well-meaning, speak for them. Advocacy informed by the voices and experience of people most affected is not only a powerful way to persuade legislators to act; it also can also result in legislation that better addresses real life needs.

Practice of Moving from Mercy to Justice

Two small urban congregations in Ohio embarked on a year of joint ministry. They shared Advent and Lenten midweek worship services and supported each other in mercy ministry projects. They also developed a new outreach and awareness effort through an annual hunger walk between the two congregations. The communities gathered one week to make signs and pass out empty bags along the route, and the following week they collected the bags full of food.

The first year of the project, the congregations focused on how to collect the most food. The second year, the congregations recognized the importance of educating their community that people of faith care about these issues and that hunger is a serious issue in our communities. They began to partner with their state public policy office. During their third year, the group spent time collecting food and educating the community but also wrote letters to their state senators on the need to solve hunger with public investment in Supplemental Nutrition Assistance Program (SNAP)[10] and school and summer lunch programs.

I have seen many church meetings where ideas are considered for a new outreach project, a way to better serve the community. Invariably, a food distribution or meals program is proposed for a first project. This inclination demonstrates an awareness of the problem of hunger in communities and shows a determination to tackle it. But often running the pantry becomes an end in itself, with a few heroic individuals putting countless hours into collecting and distributing food and meeting immediate needs.

Food security will never be achieved through just the voluntary actions of religious or civic associations. Together, they deliver less than 5 percent of the emergency food needed in the United States. Federal and state governments are much better equipped to deliver immediate relief for hungry people in the short term and to run the programs that will address long-term factors that can lift people out of poverty. If we as the church are serious about ending hunger locally and globally, it means we must engage with governments and ensure their food-security efforts are efficient, effective, adequately funded, and meeting peoples' real needs.

Fresh out of college, I served in the Lutheran Volunteer Corps running a food pantry and staffing a fledgling community organizing effort in Jersey City, New Jersey. In the shadow of the booming luxury housing developing along the waterfront, I followed up with pantry clients left out of what was called "the gold coast," visiting them in dark apartments where roaches swarmed the walls, asking how else the church could support them beyond providing food. The congregation moved into faith-based community organizing, learning the practices that raised up local leaders from our food pantry clients and congregation members, training them to use their collective power to bring about social change, analyze issues, and speak to elected officials in powerful and persuasive ways. I experienced the power and determination of people of faith to name and collectively address sources of oppression and suffering, and how engaged congregations grew in their sense of identity and mission in the process.

Scripture teaches God's call to charity and justice, not an either-or but a both-and. Luther's powerful question, "What does this mean?" is a catechetical tool we can apply when we encounter suffering in humans, other species, or all of creation. Will we address just the symptoms

10. The Supplemental Nutrition Assistance Program (SNAP) is a federally funded program that provides financial assistance to people living in or near poverty. Eligibility for benefits is determined by individual states, which administer the program.

(hunger), or will we ask after the causes of it and then target the policies and practices that can lead to greater justice through addressing equality in education, fair housing, sentencing reform, respectful treatment of returning citizens, and more? For each ministry of mercy we run, we can also ask, "what does this mean?" and see what God may ask of us in response.

Practice Ecumenical and Interreligious Action

Faith Action Network (FAN), the ELCA state public policy office in Washington State, conducts faith-based organizing through a statewide network of over 140 advocating faith communities. The Tri-Cities FAN chapter in the southeastern part of the state includes two ELCA congregations, one United Church of Christ (UCC) congregation, and one mosque. The four congregations joined a statewide initiative to end the state's legal financial obligations system, which incarcerated people unable to pay outstanding debts. The congregations conducted effective joint advocacy by conducting standing vigils in courtrooms while wearing bright yellow T-shirts imprinted with "God's Work. Our Hands" in a silent protest of the practice, and through supporting legislation to require judicial consideration of ability to pay upon being sentenced. The legislation was passed the following session.

Lutherans are deeply committed to joining ecumenical and interreligious partners in activities that range from local ministry collaboration through formal dialogues. What is less well known is the extent to which the ELCA collaborates with faith-based partners to bring about social change. In Washington, DC, more than sixty faith-based groups join forces through the Washington Interfaith Staff Community with more than twenty working groups that collaborate, strategize, and engage with Congress on issues including criminal justice reform, the environment, money in politics, and more. Very often, the same "ask" is created and shared by Jewish, Muslim, Christian, and other groups through their own networks, multiplying impact by speaking with one voice as the faith community.

God's gift of wisdom and call to do justice are not limited by denomination or faith tradition. Congregations often partner locally for worship and service. Partnering for advocacy invites new kinds of work together, including conversation about theological convictions, priorities, and hopes for the common good that can be achieved by acting together. Joint action by faith leaders attracts notice and makes an impact. A letter to the editor of your local newspaper signed by a Jewish, a Muslim, and a Christian, or visits by representatives of different congregations lets legislators know there is broad and diverse support for a bill.

Practice of Testimony

A young woman returned from her first visit to her state senator's office. She was concerned about a bill that would affect access to health care for many people, including members of her family. She had gone in armed with facts and figures about why ensuring people with low incomes can access health care makes good sense for the economy. But she found herself speaking instead about why caring for the health of others was part of her Christian faith. She said that just as Jesus sought out those suffering in body, mind, and spirit, we as a society need to work so that all people can be made whole. She reflected that she was exhilarated by the experience. "I spoke about my faith in a way I never have in public before. It was exciting to put into words what I really believe the gospel says and to do what God wants me to by speaking up."

Advocates have told me that faith-based advocacy has been key to their learning to testify to their faith. Proclamation for social change requires engaging in new ways with Scripture, examining what one truly believes and what our Lutheran tradition may add to it. Proclamation speaks to understanding that "the God who justifies calls us to do justice."[11] This is who God is, and therefore who we are, living in grateful response to God's love and mercy. Heeding God's call leads us to testify, "Here I stand!" on an issue that affects my neighbor or community.

Testimony does not take place only in halls of power with policy makers. There are opportunities for speaking up in our daily lives—so-called water-cooler advocacy at work, discussions at school, and posts on social media—that correct inaccurate and/or unjust narratives. During recent debates about immigration Lutherans have told me that while they aren't usually comfortable speaking up, they felt compelled to address coworkers and fellow congregants who demonized or portrayed migrants as dangerous criminals. They testified to the God who bids us to show hospitality to strangers, and they spoke as members of a church that values newcomers, resettles refugees, and accompanies migrants.

---

11. ELCA, *Church in Society*, 3.

A VISION FOR FAITHFUL CITIZENSHIP

The first confirmation class I ever taught gathered before the altar to rehearse the liturgy for their confirmation. We reviewed each line of the affirmation they would make in the presence of the congregation:

> *to live among God's faithful people,*
> *to hear the word of God and share in the Lord's supper,*
> *to proclaim the good news of God in Christ through word and deed,*
> *to serve all people, following the example of Jesus . . .*[12]

The confirmands nodded as they heard each of the lines, until we came to the final affirmation, "to strive for justice and peace in all the earth." One girl's eye widened and she protested, "God doesn't really expect us to do that! That's impossible!"

I present and teach about baptism as a call to advocacy, highlighting the fifth and final phrase of the covenant declaration to "strive for justice and peace in all the earth." But it is not the only portion of the affirmation rite that relates to the Christian call to social impact and social change. Our baptismal affirmations are interconnected, resting on and reinforcing one another in the life of discipleship. Each speaks to a different facet of our role as Christians in the world and supports a different aspect of the public dimensions of faithful citizenship.

The essays in this volume provide resources for teaching and practicing our baptismal vows to form citizen disciples for a life of public witness. In conversation with ELCA social teaching documents, these resources can help move us out of the huddle and into the places where the cross casts its shadow and where God's people and creation suffer.

Along with Carter Lindberg, we strive for justice and peace when we affirm that the church has a role through the preached Word in addressing and rebuking, when necessary, the actions of those who govern. If that striving is not built on the foundation of our social teaching, the grounding of a theological foundation and direction, the church will tend to take on the mores of the civil religion of its context. Without a confession of faith, the church will have little to say in a time of crisis. Read this chapter alongside the ELCA's social statements *The Church in Society: A Lutheran Perspective* and *For Peace in God's World*.

---

12. *Evangelical Lutheran Worship* (Minneapolis: Augsburg Fortress, 2006), 236.

Kirsi Stjerna highlights the Christian toleration of and participation in the horrors of the Nazi-led Holocaust. As people who hear the Word and share in the Eucharist, our public voice needs to begin in confession, acknowledging complicity in the systems of oppression, poverty, or environmental degradation that we are confronting, and tying our witness to the presence of the reconciling Christ in the world. Read her chapter alongside the ELCA's social statement *For Peace in God's World*.

The task of "living among God's faithful people" includes what Mary Jane Haemig's essay lifts up as the power of Christian education to inspire ordinary people for faith-filled public witness. Christian education is not only forming God's faithful people for life in the church but also catechesis that equips the disciples to act in the world. Read this reflection alongside the ELCA's social statement *Our Calling in Education*.

Wanda Deifelt recalls the deep concern Jesus had for the wholeness of human bodies that is echoed in Luther's concern for human thriving and the church's role in bringing healing. "Serving all people, following the command and example of Jesus" includes embodying his care for those hurting in body, mind, and spirit. Read this chapter alongside the ELCA's social statement *Caring for Health: A Shared Endeavor*.

"Proclaiming the Good News of Jesus Christ" advocates naming sinful structures that disrupt God's intention for human flourishing and Christ's reconciliation. Anthony Bateza urges going beyond "bland appeals to baptism" as a source for unity when it ignores the sin of racism. Through conversation with Luther and James Baldwin, he connects confronting personal racism with dismantling racist structures and institutions, including in government and public policy. Read his chapter alongside the ELCA's social statement *Freed in Christ: Race, Ethnicity, and Culture*.

Advocacy is the stewardship of our citizenship that incorporates God's love for all the world, Christ's command to love our neighbor, and the positive view Lutherans hold of government into our public faith witness. As Conrad Braaten and Paul Wee note in the introduction to this book, if we don't advocate according to our faith convictions and deep-rooted social teaching, other voices that may not give priority to vulnerable people or the integrity of creation will prevail. We may (and do!) win on policy issues, but our goal is deeper: a life of determined witness to both the crosses of suffering in our midst and the presence of the resurrected Christ in those places of suffering, calling us to stand with and for our neighbor and the healing of all creation.

Faithful citizenship is resurrection work, an act of hope confessing publicly that the God of hope is active in all spheres of our lives, even in the world of public policy and the machinery of the legislative process.

God is at work here through those who serve in public office, but God is also powerfully present through our actions to bring greater peace and well-being to the world. When we act on the inspiration of these essays as faithful citizens, we can and will make a difference, acting in hope on behalf of God's creative, reconciling, and redemptive presence.

Discussion Questions

CHAPTER 1: RECLAIMING LUTHER'S PUBLIC WITNESS ON CHURCH, STATE, AND WAR

Carter Lindberg

1. Lindberg argues that Christians in the United States have focused on "private morality" (the kinds of personal behaviors that individuals practice in their daily lives) and lost sight of "public morality" (the ways that society, government, and other institutions are structured). What might be some examples of times the church has focused on private morality and neglected public morality? Do you think Lindberg is right? Why or why not?

2. Lindberg opens his chapter by citing several authors who believe that Lutheran faith has a significant role to play in American culture and religion. What positive contributions can Luther and the Lutheran church make to culture, politics, and society today? How might "a good dose of Luther" help shape American public life?

3. Lindberg quotes Michael Laffin, who calls Luther's politics "a politics lived out of faith in the God who alone judges and justifies." What do you think this kind of politics looks like? What does it mean to be active in the world, knowing that salvation comes from God alone, and not from a political, economic, or social institution?

4. Lindberg describes the ways a few European Lutherans drew on their heritage to resist Nazism and totalitarianism in the

twentieth century. What resources from the Lutheran tradition helped justify their resistance? What does their witness mean for Lutherans around the world today?

5. Looking back at Lindberg's chapter, what do you think are the purposes of government, from a Lutheran perspective? What are government's limits?

6. Lindberg cites Luther's call to preachers not only to preach the gospel but also to "unmask hidden injustice" and hold political authorities accountable to justice. What responsibilities do both clergy and laypeople have in holding political authorities accountable? What are some healthy ways this can be—or is—done?

7. What lessons about Martin Luther's theology and politics did you find most surprising in the chapter?

CHAPTER 2: LUTHERAN FAITH: REBELLION AND RESPONSIBILITY

Kirsi I. Stjerna

1. Stjerna reminds readers of the feisty, radical side of Luther's Reformation, especially in the face of the injustice of powerful political and religious leaders. What can the modern church today learn from Luther's model of radical, prophetic engagement with authority?

2. In what ways has the church been complicit in injustice? In what ways has the church been a prophetic agent of change in society?

3. How does the freedom Christians have in Christ obligate the church to "do something, do anything" in the face of human suffering, and the suffering of all creation?

4. In its 1994 statement on Lutheran-Jewish relations, the Evangelical Lutheran Church in America (ELCA) affirmed that "we who bear [Luther's] name must with pain acknowledge also Luther's anti-Judaic diatribes and the violent recommendations of his later writings against the Jews." How can the Lutheran church today find value in Luther's theology while not excusing or ignoring the deadly prejudices that Luther also

taught? In an era of increasing anti-Semitism and anti-Judaism, what special responsibilities do Lutherans today have to their Jewish neighbors?

5. Stjerna notes that Luther and his contemporaries had few occasions to interact with their Jewish neighbors and get to know them. How can building stronger relationships across ethnic, religious, racial, and cultural lines help inspire justice and reduce prejudice and violence? What are the obstacles people today face to building these relationships? How can the church help overcome them?

6. Respond to Stjerna's questions in her chapter: "What is the meaning of Christ to us? How shall we walk in the footsteps of Christ and express the core of his message? Compassion and freedom and equality—do these words resonate with how we understand what being a follower of Christ means?"

7. What lessons about Martin Luther's teachings, theology, or politics did you find most surprising in the chapter?

CHAPTER 3: RECLAIMING THE EMPOWERMENT OF ORDINARY PEOPLE

Mary Jane Haemig

1. What are some of the ways Luther empowered ordinary people, according to Haemig? What reflections of this do you see in the modern church today? Where do you see the empowerment of ordinary people in the church today?

2. In what ways do (or might) catechism lessons in the church today empower Christians to be responsible citizens?

3. In what ways are laypeople in congregations today actively holding preachers (or any authority, inside or outside the church) to account?

4. Haemig notes that Luther's views regarding the education of girls and women were revolutionary. How can access to education for everyone benefit society as a whole?

5. Do modern worship practices meet the Reformers' goal of empowering the "ordinary people"? Why or why not?

6. Haemig writes, "The Lutheran Reformation had significant

and long-lasting consequences for ordinary people who had been marginalized and, in many respects, forgotten in church and society." Who are the "forgotten people" today who are marginalized in church and society? How can Lutherans today draw on the Lutheran tradition to counteract marginalization of themselves and their neighbors?

7. What lessons about Martin Luther's teachings, theology, or politics did you find most surprising in the chapter?

CHAPTER 4: RECLAIMING AN ETHIC OF CARE IN LUTHER'S THEOLOGY OF EMBODIMENT

Wanda Deifelt

1. How does Jesus show concern for people's bodily needs? How does the church today reflect this same concern?

2. Deifelt writes, "When human bodies are respected and honored, justice abounds." How can showing concern and respect for bodies—all bodies—help justice abound? How can ignoring the body and focusing exclusively on the soul lead to injustice or violence?

3. What does it mean to consider the body a gift of God? How does the church help people of faith see this truth?

4. In what ways are Christians called to be "justice-seeking beings"? What resources from Luther does Deifelt highlight for readers?

5. How does Deifelt's understanding of "care" broaden the definition of the term? What does it mean to care for the physical and spiritual needs of the neighbor?

6. What are some of the ways bodies are mistreated or devalued in society and culture today? How can the church witness to a belief that "the body is a beautiful and noble creation of God"?

7. What lessons about Martin Luther's teachings, theology, or politics did you find most surprising in the chapter?

CHAPTER 5: RECLAIMING THE LEGACIES OF MARTIN LUTHER AND JAMES BALDWIN IN FIGHTING RACISM

Anthony Bateza

1. What are some of the differences between seeing racism solely as the obvious actions or words of an individual and seeing racism as the discriminatory ways social institutions are structured? How does Bateza help expand the definition of racism?

2. Name some reasons it is challenging to examine Luther's writings for ways to address an issue such as racism today. What might be gained by looking to Luther to speak to modern issues?

3. How is baptism part of the "story" you tell about yourself? How is faith part of your identity as a neighbor, family member, worker, citizen, and so forth?

4. What obligations do people of faith have to intervene against public sins such as racism?

5. Bateza notes that, according to Luther, holding government accountable is one of the duties Christians owe to the government and to God. In what ways can holding government accountable and working for racial justice reflect faith in God's care for the world?

6. In what ways are churches today sites where people of faith can tell and hear "as much of the truth as one can bear, and then a little more," particularly when it comes to the hard truth of racism? Whose voices need to be heard for this truth to be told?

7. What lessons about Martin Luther's teachings, theology, or politics did you find most surprising in the chapter?

CHAPTER 6: GOD'S WORD SPOKEN PUBLICLY, BOLDLY, AND HONESTLY

Amy Reumann

1. Thinking of Reumann's chapter and the other chapters in this book, how would you describe the difference between a public

gospel expressed through advocacy and private devotion that separates faith and public action?

2. What does it mean to be an advocate? When have you seen your church acting as an advocate for people in need in your community?

3. How does "mercy" differ from "justice"? How can advocacy for justice complement mercy ministries that meet immediate needs?

4. How can the church be a site of reconciliation and unity amid political divisiveness, according to Reumann? Why is it important for the church to take on this role?

5. What are some of the challenges you see in having conversations about public policy in your congregation? How might leaders in the congregation help address these challenges and foster dialogue?

6. What is the difference between doing advocacy *for* someone and doing advocacy *with* someone? Why is the latter more effective, according to Reumann?

7. What is one civil, legal, or political need in your community that could be addressed through your congregation's advocacy? What steps could your congregation take—or has it taken—to advocate on this issue?

Contributors

Anthony Bateza, assistant professor of religion, St. Olaf College, received his BS from Iowa State, MDiv from Lutheran School of Theology at Chicago, and PhD from Princeton Seminary. He is a specialist in Martin Luther, moral theology, and Christian ethics. His research examines Luther's understanding of human agency and his relationship with the virtue tradition. His other scholarly interests include the broader Augustinian tradition, the impact of Luther's thought on nineteenth-century philosophy, and questions of race, identity, and social justice. Anthony is an ordained pastor in the Evangelical Lutheran Church in America (ELCA).

Conrad Braaten, a pastor of the Evangelical Lutheran Church in America, is responsible for initiating the Forgotten Luther project. He retired in 2012 from his position as senior pastor of the Lutheran Church of the Reformation in Washington, DC. Prior to this, Braaten was on the staff of the ELCA's Division for Congregational Life in the program areas of urban ministry and congregational social ministry and for more than a decade was a member of the USA Committee of the Lutheran World Federation's Caribbean-Haiti Program. He has coordinated and led more than twenty-five educational immersions to countries in the Caribbean, Central America, and South America. He has written on biblical and theological themes and continues to engage in programs designed to equip pastors and laypeople in methods of advocacy with those who have been denied justice.

Ryan P. Cumming is the program director of hunger education for ELCA World Hunger. He received his MA and PhD in theology from Loyola University Chicago and his BA from Capital University. His area of research focuses on Christian social ethics, particularly issues related to economics, just war theory, and social justice. He has taught religious studies and theology at Loyola and Central Michigan University, and his writings include *The African American Challenge to Just War Theory: A Christian Approach* (Palgrave Macmillan, 2013). He was also a contributor to *The Forgotten Luther: Reclaiming the Social-Economic Dimension of the Reformation* (Lutheran University Press, 2016).

Wanda Deifelt, professor of religion at Luther College, received her BA from Faculdade de Teologia (São Leopoldo, Brazil), MTS from Garrett-Evangelical Theological Seminary (Evanston, Illinois), and PhD from Northwestern University. From Brazil, she served as vice president of the seminary and provost of the graduate program in theology at Ecola Superior de Teologia, in São Leopoldo, Brazil (the largest Lutheran Seminary in Latin America). An ordained pastor of the Evangelical Lutheran Church in Brazil, she is currently a member of the bilateral Roman Catholic and Lutheran dialogue, appointed by the Pontifical Council for the Promotion of Christian Unity and the Lutheran World Federation.

Mary Jane Haemig, professor of church history and director of the Reformation Research Program at Luther Seminary (St. Paul, Minnesota), received her JD, MTS, and ThD degrees from Harvard University. She specializes in Reformation studies with particular attention to preaching, catechesis, and prayer. She edited volume 4, *Pastoral Writings*, of *The Annotated Luther* (Fortress Press) and is coeditor and contributor to *Dictionary of Luther and the Lutheran Tradition* (Baker Academic, 2017). She is a member of the continuation committee for the International Luther Research Congress.

Carter Lindberg, professor emeritus of church history, Boston University School of Theology, received his BA from Augustana College (Illinois), MDiv from the Lutheran School of Theology at Chicago, and PhD from the University of Iowa School of Religion. His academic interest is Reformation studies, with particular focus on Luther's contributions to social welfare. His publications range from *Beyond Charity: Reformation Initiatives for the Poor* (Fortress Press, 1993) to *The European Reformations*, 2nd ed. (Wiley-Blackwell, 2010).

Amy Reumann serves as director of advocacy for the Evangelical Lutheran Church in America in Washington, DC. She is an ELCA pastor and has served congregations in New Jersey and Wisconsin, as assistant to the bishop for urban ministry in Milwaukee, in the Lutheran Office for World Community at the United Nations, and Lutheran advocacy ministry in Pennsylvania. Amy is a graduate of Muhlenberg College, received her MDiv from the Lutheran School of Theology at Chicago and the Theologisches Seminar in Leipzig, Germany, and was awarded a master's in Christian spirituality and spiritual direction at the General Theological Seminary, New York City.

Kirsi I. Stjerna is the First Lutheran, Los Angeles/Southwest Synod Professor of Lutheran History and Theology (Chair) at Pacific Lutheran Theological Seminary of California Lutheran University in Berkeley, and also serves on the core doctoral faculty of the Graduate Theological Union at Berkeley and as a docent at Helsinki University. She received her PhD from Boston University after finishing a master's of theology degree in Helsinki and studies in Rome. Ordained in Finland, she is on the clergy roster of the Evangelical Lutheran Church in both Finland and the United States. Her publications include *Women and the Reformation* (2009), *Martin Luther, the Bible and the Jews* (2012, with Brooks Schramm), and *The Annotated Luther*, vols. 1–6 (co–general editor and a volume editor).

Paul Wee has been adjunct professor at the Elliott School of International Affairs, George Washington University, Washington, DC. Wee was assistant general secretary for international affairs and human rights of the Geneva-based Lutheran World Federation from 1986 to 1994 and senior pastor of the Church of the Reformation in Washington, DC, following this. He has served as International Theological Director of the Luther Center in Wittenberg, Germany, and program officer in the Religion and Peacemaking unit of the United Sates Institute of Peace, working primarily on interfaith conflict resolution in Nigeria and Colombia.

Acknowledgments

We would like to express gratitude to the many congregations of the ELCA that participated in the initial study project *The Forgotten Luther: Reclaiming the Social-Economic Dimension of the Reformation.* It was their enthusiastic response to the study of that neglected issue that occasions the present investigation into the related theme that is the focus of this study, *Reclaiming the Church's Public Witness.*

This congregational study project is part of a global effort that seeks to bring the public witness of the Reformation to bear on the mission of the church today. At its heart is a commitment on the part of Lutheran churches around the world to address the *causes* of world hunger and poverty from a biblical and confessional perspective. This focus on the factors that have created and perpetuated the unacceptably wide chasm that divides the wealthy few from the great masses of humanity is central to this study and action project. The international study, "Radicalizing Reformation: Provoked by the Bible and Today's Crises," is led by noted Lutheran theologian Dr. Ulrich Duchrow of Heidelberg, Germany. Leading this project in North America is well-known theologian and former Director of the Department for Theology and Studies of the Lutheran World Federation (LWF), Dr. Karen Bloomquist.

For generous financial support for this project we want to thank:

- Saint Luke Lutheran Church, in Silver Spring, Maryland, led by Pr. Connie Miller. We are especially grateful that this congregation was moved to make a major financial contribution toward the January 2018 symposium that produced this book;

- the Metropolitan Washington, DC, Synod of the Evangelical Lutheran Church in America (ELCA,) led by Bishop Richard Graham;

- the Global Mission Team of the Synod, led by Rev. Robert Allard;

- Arnie and Ruth Sorenson for their ongoing support to the church's mission; and

- ELCA World Hunger.

For the symposium itself we are grateful for support provided through a Hunger Education and Networking Grant.

We want to express thanks to Pr. Michael Wilker and the Church of the Reformation in Washington, DC, for again hosting the symposium that served as the public platform for the initial presentation of these essays. For their dedication and tireless work in preparing for that event, we are immensely grateful to the Forgotten Luther Working Group, especially to Mrs. Karen Cowden; Mr. John Hagood; Ms. Kathy Tobias; Mr. Al Anderson; Mr. Scott Binde; the congregation's treasurer, Ms. Suzanne Hazard; and others who volunteered hours of service, as well as to the Church of the Reformation's accomplished organist and Director of Music and the Arts, Mr. Paul Leavitt.

Accompanying this study from the outset has been Mr. Scott Tunseth, senior acquiring editor at Fortress Press. For Scott's encouragement and wise counsel throughout, we are most grateful. Congregational groups that desire to participate in this study will be aided by video recordings of the original lectures as well as video interviews with the presenters. We are indebted to Mr. Wes Browning of Sema Films, Atlanta, for these expert professional services. A very special word of thanks is due the creative leader of ELCA's World Hunger Education program, Dr. Ryan Cumming. In our estimation, few people have done more than he to equip church members for knowledgeable participation in world hunger efforts. We are pleased that Ryan, whose multifaceted ministry to end hunger is well-known throughout the church, has agreed to edit the material contained in this book. All who have worked on this project agreed at once with Ryan's suggestion that any royalties received from the sale of the book be designated for the ELCA World Hunger Program.

This study itself is dedicated to two members of the original Forgotten Luther Working Group who have provided inspiration and creative leadership over several years. Ms. Amy Northcutt, mother of two young children, died unexpectedly of a brain tumor in May 2017. Amy was an accomplished lawyer and chief information officer for the National Science Foundation (NSF). Rev. Philip Anderson, who worked tirelessly for peace and reconciliation in Central America on behalf of the

Lutheran World Federation (LWF), died from cancer in August 2017. Both of these colleagues were committed to the knowledgeable expression of the church's witness in the political realm.

Paul Wee
Conrad Braaten